The 12 Steps Unplugged

The 12 Steps Unplugged

A Young Person's
Guide to
Alcoholics Anonymous

JOHN R.

Formerly titled *Big Book Unplugged*

HazeLDeN®

Hazelden
Center City, Minnesota 55012
hazelden.org

ISBN: 978-1-61649-110-9

Editor's note: All references to the Big Book are to the fourth edition of *Alcoholics Anonymous*.

Cover design by David Spohn
Typesetting by BookMobile Design and Publishing Services

To Audrey, Pat, Jerry, Ralph, and Rich,
who patiently showed me the way.

CONTENTS

ACKNOWLEDGMENTS

I would like to thank Richard Solly at Hazelden for his early interest in this project and Becky Post for seeing it through with her clear editor's vision.

Thanks also to all of the brave souls I've met in the Fellowship throughout the world—without you, I wouldn't be here, and this book wouldn't have been possible.

Last but not least, thanks to my Higher Power, who makes it all possible.

INTRODUCTION

Know how to keep a secret from an alcoholic? Put it in the Big Book.

We alcoholics and addicts are reluctant to read the Big Book, which is officially titled *Alcoholics Anonymous*. Maybe it's because the book seems so big and was written long ago. For whatever reason, it's too bad that the wisdom in the Big Book doesn't reach more alcoholics.

This guide is intended to help you discover the Big Book's hidden treasures. Think of it as a guidebook for a trip you're about to take. This guide points out sights of interest and things not to miss. It's not a substitute for the trip itself. Rather, it will help you make the most of your trip.

Along the way, you might realize the Big Book isn't so big after all. It's broken into two main parts. The first part, the text of chapters 1–11, is only 164 pages. The forty-two personal stories in the second part give the book its bulk. The first eleven chapters of this guide correspond with the first part of the Big Book. Each chapter in this book breaks down the main insights of the corresponding Big Book chapter. The remainder of this guide is devoted to understanding the personal stories better. I've picked eight stories that I thought might speak to you. These people started using when they were young, just like you and me.

I suggest you try this: First, read the chapter or personal story in the Big Book without worrying too much about what doesn't make sense. Then, read the corresponding chapter in the guidebook. Finally, go back and read the Big Book chapter again. You'll be amazed at how much more you discover upon this reading.

Soon you'll be well traveled in the secrets of *Alcoholics Anonymous* and understand the solution it offers you. My wishes for a satisfying journey.

1

BILL'S STORY

There's no problem that can't be made
worse by picking up a drink.

The Big Book begins like an old movie. We meet Bill, a high-flying, gin-loving Wall Street guy making millions during the Roaring Twenties. But, you wonder, what does this have to do with me?

Bill is a promising guy with a bright future. He crashes and burns because of his insatiable appetite for alcohol. I was one of those guys, too, only many years later. I was a pot-smoking kid from the suburbs. I washed dishes for spending money.

I first got drunk at fourteen. In the kitchen of a friend's house, I guzzled bourbon stolen from his parents' liquor cabinet.

Like Bill, I'd heard strong warnings about alcohol, especially from my parents. They'd told me about my grandfather, a promising salesman who ended up a skid-row drunk. That first night I drank, giddy with the alcohol in me, I walked a straight line along the pattern in the kitchen carpet. "See—alcohol won't affect me the way it does others." So began an early delusion about being invincible.

Bill defended alcohol. When his wife voiced her concerns, he rationalized that men of genius had come up with their best stuff when drunk; that the philosophers thought their deepest thoughts under the influence. I remember saying the same sort of thing while smoking pot in another friend's basement.

Any of this sounding familiar?

Find the Common Ground

Here's the first secret to making some sense of the Big Book: Look for what you have in common. Then you'll be able to hear what it has to say.

When Bill's friends confronted his drinking, he argued with them. When my parents confronted me with bottles or bags they found, I lied and denied. We got the same result—we hurt those who cared about us. We put our drugs before our loved ones.

Bill's consequences mounted. He could no longer choose when he wanted to drink; he needed alcohol to function.

I felt the same way. I couldn't go to a party without using. I could barely walk down the school hallway without being high. I needed to drink or smoke dope to calm my emotional shakes.

Yet, and here's the crazy part, Bill and I both believed we could still control our use. That, my friend, is called denial.

Suddenly, Bill woke up. He knew he had to quit, so he did. Then, someone offered him a drink. He took it but couldn't stop. He came home drunk. He proved he didn't have control— once he started drinking, he couldn't stop himself.

That was me. Light a joint, I had to finish it. A toke or two wouldn't do. What was the point of that? I wanted to get high.

Bill repeated a cycle of resolve, drink, remorse, drink. Me too. I remember puking my guts out the morning after a night of drinking, hugging the toilet and swearing I'd never drink like that again. Then I'd wind up drunk that night! Of course, the next day I'd feel shitty about myself. Then I'd have to get high or drunk. My life cycled down the toilet.

Nowhere to Run

Bill tried geographics, moving from the city to the country and from the country to the city. He brought his problem with him wherever he went. I switched from school to school. But, what do you know? I kept partying. My problem dogged me.

Bill details financial disasters, something I didn't experience as a teenager living with my parents. But Bill had moral, mental, and physical consequences I could relate to.

He stole from his wife's purse. I stole dope from my friend. I knew it was wrong to steal, but I sacrificed my values to get a fix. Whenever I violated my moral code, I felt like scum. That's how alcohol and drug abuse quietly corrodes your self-esteem.

All I wanted to do was get wasted, blasted, loaded, stoned, bombed, shit-faced. Ever think about those terms and what they're saying? When I got wasted, I ended up wasting my life.

Bill believed self-knowledge would allow him to drink without the consequences. Ha! That's like saying, "Knowing I've got diarrhea is enough for me to make it stop." Good luck.

Bill became a slave to his drug of choice. He couldn't control alcohol; it controlled him. And it wasn't a kind master. Nor was my drug of choice—marijuana. It doled out some nasty punishments.

Camp Detox

My last night using, I went to a party in the woods. I was seventeen with a bottle of whiskey tucked in my jacket. I'd quit smoking dope—had been high only three times in the past two weeks—but got stoned that night after a few whiskey sours.

The cops busted our party. I refused to leave. We were there first, I argued. "Uh-oh," my friends said. "Come on, John, let's get out of here."

Nope. In my drunken and stoned stupor, I felt justified. All of my pent-up anger at authority spewed out. The cops hauled me downtown.

I blacked out, then passed out. Came to in detox.

But here's how screwed up my thinking really was: I figured if I didn't tell them my name, I couldn't get into trouble. I'd break out of the locked unit, hitchhike home even though I didn't know where I was, and sneak back into my bed before my parents realized I hadn't come home.

My plan didn't work. At 5:45 A.M. I finally told the captors my name. They called my parents, who had been up all night worrying. I stayed four days at Camp Detox. And my recovery began.

The God Stuff

For Bill, an old drinking buddy showed up sober. He asked Bill if he could share with him how he had done it. The guy had gotten religion and followed some basic steps.

Before you freak out about the God stuff, listen to what happened to him. (We'll talk about God hang-ups in chapter 4.) Bill had some reservations and suspicions himself. But his friend suggested, "Why don't you choose your own conception of God?" He wasn't trying to cram a belief down Bill's throat. Instead, he suggested that Bill try to find God in his own experience and out of his own understanding.

That idea helped me when I met the Twelve Steps in treatment, which followed detox. I was angry at a God who had not delivered on my prayers. I had rejected the God my parents had raised me with. But when I found out I could choose my own belief, it put the responsibility back on me and took away the need to rebel. I started my spiritual exploration.

Bill's friend told him that "God had done for him what he could not do for himself." Like Bill, he had tried to quit on his own and failed. But with God's grace he had gotten sober, cleaned up his life, and found peace. Whoa! Bill saw a miracle sitting before him. He wanted what this guy had.

All he had to do was be willing to believe in a power greater than himself. He became willing to have God with him, and God showed up. He humbly offered himself to God. In other words, he turned himself over to the care and direction of a loving God.

I, too, realized that I had placed my faith in alcohol and drugs. That had not led to my salvation. Detox was no paradise. I was ready to try something else. In treatment, I met people who had been addicted to drugs and alcohol but had broken free. They had a peace and ease that I wanted. I was willing to do what these people—we called them counselors—suggested.

They pointed out where my way had gotten me. "If that's where you want to be," they said, "don't change a thing. But if you want what we've got, try trusting God, however you conceive of him."

Bill's friend promised him that he'd enter into a new relationship with his Creator. My counselors basically promised the same thing. Not only would this plan of action work to keep us clean and sober, it would be rewarding.

There was, of course, a hitch. Here's what we had to do:

- give up being self-centered
- care about others
- respect their wants and feelings

- think beyond ourselves
- reach out to help other alcoholics and addicts still struggling
- remain humble and willing
- stay honest in everything

Our reward for these efforts? A second chance to a happy life.

It wasn't, however, happily ever after. Bill felt plagued by self-pity and resentment. I felt haunted by fears and resentment. But there was a way out. Bill struck upon it in the fellowship of Alcoholics Anonymous, which he founded without knowing what he was doing. He merely reached out to other alcoholics. He eventually wrote the Twelve Steps, which can serve as our blueprint for living. The Twelve Steps also help us deal with fear, self-pity, and resentment. (More on that in the chapters ahead.)

Bill also tells us that getting clean and sober can be fun. Life on this side of the drugs doesn't have to be dull. That was good news to me. Years later, I can say, it's true. What will you have to say about it years from now?

2

THERE IS A SOLUTION

Alcoholism is the only disease that tries to
convince you that you don't have it.

So what's the purpose of the Big Book? It's simple: The Big
Book provides solutions to what we couldn't fix. It tells us how
to recover from the seemingly hopeless condition of addiction.
Our own efforts at fixing things didn't work. Yet, this chapter
promises that we're capable of taking steps that will work.

Even though the Big Book was written decades ago, its
advice still holds true today. It has stood the test of time. The
solutions offered in the Big Book work for people of all ages
and all walks of life. They formed the foundation of the AA
Fellowship.

Radical Thinking
The authors call alcoholism an illness in chapter 2. That was
radical thinking sixty years ago when the book was written.
Back then, society viewed an alcoholic as a moral failure.
Alcoholism was treated with ignorance and misunderstanding. Thankfully, much has changed. Today, many people know
alcoholism or drug addiction is a disease. Like other diseases,

alcoholism can be passed down in families. Likewise, alcoholics and addicts need medical treatment.

The solution to recovery remains the same now as years ago. Even with the advance in society's attitudes, no one understands the addict better than another addict. Perhaps that's because our illness is unlike other illnesses. It tends to hurt and anger those around us rather than stir up sympathy and compassion. We need that special understanding offered by other addicts, or our fellows. Those who have found "the solution" can usually "get through" to using alcoholics or addicts because they understand in a way few others can. That's the bond upon which our Twelve Step Fellowship is based and by which the message spreads.

Chapter 2 tells us that at some point addicts can no longer stop drinking or drugging once they've taken that first drink or hit. They've lost control. The drugs now control them.

Willpower won't work. Our resolve isn't strong enough. Staying clean can't happen through some trick of the mind. The addiction is too powerful, and we lose the power of choice.

The disease seems to invade every fiber of our being, infecting us even when we're straight. Despite a string of negative consequences and every good reason to quit, we persist:

- We drink to get drunk; we use to get high.
- Our personality changes when intoxicated.
- We have a "positive genius" for getting wasted at just the wrong moment.
- We become dishonest and selfish.
- We protect our supply.

Yet, most of us were not ready to give up alcohol and drugs. We tried to find some trick to drink or use without the consequences. We've got a name for that too: denial.

Why do addicts act like this? Why, when they know from experience the problems that using causes, do they use again?

That's the wrong question. We can't answer it. Truth be told, most of us have no idea why we kept using.

The better question is, "What do I have to do to recover from this seemingly hopeless condition?" That's where the solution comes in.

Simple, but Not Easy

By now, you're no doubt asking, what the heck is this "solution" they keep talking about?

It's simple. The solution is to change. Through a spiritual experience, we overhaul our way of looking at and being in the world. We surrender our plans and submit to God's will. We turn from self-centeredness and begin a life of service to others.

It's simple, but not easy. At first, most didn't like the requirements—self-searching, leveling of pride, confession of shortcomings. Since our way hadn't worked, we were willing to try it, especially when we saw how it had worked for others.

Basically, it came down to two choices:
- follow our addiction to its bitter end, which meant insanity, incarceration, or death, or
- accept spiritual help.

There was no middle road or shortcut. It was drink until we dropped, or surrender. Stay with the problem, or embrace the solution.

The solution, we found, was nothing short of a miracle, especially considering our doubts. Surrendering to God brings relief. God can do for us what we could never do by ourselves.

Not only has God liberated us from our addiction, God has given us the grace to change our attitude and approach to life. Cutting out the drugs is just the beginning. The solution lies in applying the principles we've discovered to every aspect of our lives. (More on these principles and working the Steps in later chapters.) The solution is more than a means to quit using, it's a "design on living."

This design is drawn from the paradox that we cannot keep what we have unless we give it away. In helping others, we help ourselves. Service, particularly helping the addict who is still suffering, becomes the foundation of sobriety. In fact, our very lives depend on helping others. That gives our lives purpose. And it keeps us sober.

Instead of looking out for ourselves, we try to be useful to others. We talk to other addicts about what we know. We share our own painful experience with others who need to know they aren't alone. That can give our lives purpose. And it keeps us sober.

More God Stuff

So what's with the spiritual experience? Chapter 2 defines a spiritual experience as a new way of looking at life. We throw away old ideas and attitudes that hurt us and others.

Appendix 2, in the back of the Big Book, further describes what the authors mean by a "spiritual experience." Some people had sudden, dramatic spiritual experiences. But most people had slow, subtle transformations. Sometimes they happened so slowly that others spotted the changes before the individual was even aware of them. Eventually the individual realized that he or she no longer carried the old outlook.

These positive changes didn't occur solely through the individuals' efforts. God did for them what they couldn't do for themselves. Slowly, surely, they were transformed into happy people. Tapping into this resource—this Power greater than themselves—is the essence of spiritual experience.

The authors of the Big Book say that religion alone won't supply this vital spiritual experience. They also stress that there are many ways to tap into the spiritual source. Just as there are many paths up the same mountain, there are many ways to discover a Higher Power. The key is to be open and willing.

In fact, willingness, honesty, and open-mindedness are the keys to recovery. Willingness, honesty, and open-mindedness unlock a whole new life.

The Big Book also offers hope. We can experience a new life if we do these things:

- face our problems honestly
- keep our minds open to spiritual concepts
- beware of attitudes of intolerance and denial

Remember, sometimes the answers to our problems don't come in the form we expect. And sometimes we may be looking for ways to keep using. So be honest about your motives. And be willing to accept the help of other recovering people.

3

MORE ABOUT ALCOHOLISM

Drunkenness is nothing but voluntary madness.

Chapter 3 tells us that all alcoholics have one great obsession: to gain control over their drinking. So, too, drug addicts want to control their use.

"Normal" drinkers have no problem controlling their drinking. If they do have a problem with drugs or alcohol, they simply adjust their use, and the problem goes away.

We're not so lucky. Control remains elusive. The recurring problems prevent us from really enjoying our use. But we press on, determined that one day, we'll be in charge and have a good time. We become obsessed by the idea. That in itself shows how important drinking and drugging has become in our lives. Not really normal, is it?

Our obsession makes it tough to admit that "someday" will never come for us. But that's the first step on the road to recovery. This chapter tells us that we must fully admit we're alcoholics. We must come clean with ourselves and fess up that we fit the definition of an alcoholic: we can't control our drinking and drugging. Somewhere along the way, we lost that ability.

Not Me, I'm Different

Once we've lost that ability, nothing will bring it back. Doctors agree. Sixty years after the Big Book was written, science still hasn't found a way for addicts to regain control of their drugging. That's the simple truth about us.

Chances are, if you're one of us, you read those words and think, *Not me, I'm different. I'll prove them wrong.* Well, good luck. We tried all of the ways listed in chapter 3 and then some but found we couldn't do it.

Chapter 3 calls alcoholism a "progressive illness." This means it gets worse with time, never better. Not even prolonged periods of abstinence will turn back its progression. Once it strikes us, addiction carries us along like a raft caught in the rapids.

> Simply put, once we're an alcoholic, we're always an alcoholic. Abstinence for the addict is simply a period of remission. Pick up another drink or drug after a break—no matter how long—and the disease returns full force. We pick up where we left off. This is a progressive illness.

Our obsession that someday we'll control and enjoy our drugging is an illusion. Not even thirty years of abstinence will change our situation. It's best to abandon the obsession.

Can You Say, "Progressive Illness"?

Still not convinced? There's another test: stay clean and sober for a year. Few true alcoholics or addicts can. Fail the test, and that's another way to prove you're one of us. Catch is, even if you make it a year without any alcohol or drugs, you still haven't proven you're not an alcoholic or addict. Remember the guy sober thirty years. Once he started drinking again, he was dead in four. Can you say, "progressive illness"?

Chapter 3 of the Big Book talks about young people. Even those who hadn't been drinking long still found themselves as helpless as those who had been drinking twenty years. Addiction can happen quickly. Research has proven that the younger you are when you start drinking, the more likely you are to become addicted.

The Big Book tells us that 20 percent of AA's members are under thirty. We who are young are by no means safe from the grips of addiction. The good news is that we're also eligible to share in the solution.

Insanity

So, why, despite past problems, do we addicts use again? In a word, *insanity*.

The insanity occurs in the way we twist our thinking to justify the decision to drink or use, despite overwhelming evidence that our decision is flawed. Such thinking usually precedes a relapse. We don't slip back into our addiction by any sane means.

Chapter 3 reminds us that this twisted thinking—this insanity—is common among addicts. Remember, we're obsessed with the idea that somehow, someday we'll control and enjoy our drinking and drugging. That obsession can drive us crazy.

Chapter 3 talks about the insanity of jaywalking (crossing an intersection carelessly, such as when the light is red). Or driving the wrong way down a one-way street. It would be insane to keep driving into a lane of oncoming traffic. Well, that's how our drinking and drugging looks to others. Problem is, the ears are often the first to go. We can't hear their concerns because we're consumed by our obsession.

Some people who have had problems with drugs and alcohol can change their use. Maybe you've seen this with your classmates or other using buddies. They had consequences and cut back or quit altogether. Problem solved. But the true addict isn't so lucky.

The authors say they want to smash home this point: You can't do it by yourself. Maybe you've tried. You know. If you're one of us and honest with yourself, you'll see what they say is true.

Not Me

We meet Fred in chapter 3. He was a "not me" guy. He was confident that the problems others described couldn't happen to him. *Not me.* That state of mind can kill us. Further, if experience has shown otherwise—that we suffer the symptoms outlined here—then that state of mind is another form of insanity.

Underlying this "not me" mentality is the thought that somehow we're different from others. Those things may happen to them, but they won't happen to me. It's like believing you'll never be in a car accident. That always happens to other people, not me. It's a sort of ignorant arrogance.

Back to Fred, he drinks impulsively, with almost no thought, other than that a few drinks seem like a good idea. Bam! He's disappeared on a binge. That quick sleight of mind was all it took.

To Fred's credit, the experience taught him he had an "alcoholic mind," one prone to insanity. One prone to that flawed reasoning described earlier. One not to be trusted by itself. As AA members like to say, "My mind is like a bad neighborhood—I shouldn't go in there alone."

When Fred tells his two friends from AA how his mind tricked him, they grin. Not to laugh at him, but in recognition. They know that way of thinking—it was once their own. "Such an alcoholic mentality is a hopeless condition," they tell him.

They remind him there is a solution. They outline the spiritual remedy and "program of action." Like those before him, Fred isn't happy to learn that this "program of action" requires him to change his thinking and attitude. Yet, also like those others, his story has a happy ending. By the end of the chapter, his life has become more satisfying and useful to others.

The chapter concludes with a summary supported by the physician's opinion: Given their insane mentality, addicts are defenseless against drugs. Only a Higher Power can save them from their own thinking. Therein lies the solution.

4

WE AGNOSTICS

Don't believe everything you think.

First of all, what is an agnostic? An agnostic is someone who isn't sure whether he or she believes in God. And what's an atheist? An atheist doesn't believe in God.

God. The very word gives some the heebie-jeebies. We see that word pop up on the page and we want to close the book. We want nothing to do with God.

Even those more comfortable with the idea of God carry some baggage. I was one of those. I was raised by devout parents, but I grew angry at God over a string of prayers not answered to my liking. Eventually, I shifted my faith from God to pot and alcohol. Though they let me down as well, I was too immersed in my addiction to find my way back to God.

Many readers of the Big Book feel uneasy, even defiant, toward God. Chapter 4 intends to calm some of those fears and ease that resistance.

It's helpful to remember that the Big Book encourages you to find your own concept of God. The authors of the Big Book weren't speaking about the Jewish God, the Christian God, the Muslim God, or any other God of organized world religion. Their talk of God had nothing to do with organized religion—which is something separate altogether. When they said "God," they weren't saying, "This God." They were saying, "Your God—whoever that might be."

It helped me to know I didn't have to believe exactly what others believed. Perhaps that will help you as well. You can believe in your God—whoever that might be.

Still, the people who don't believe in a God or Higher Power of any sort find themselves in a tough spot. The Big Book does say, after all, that addiction will consume us if we don't accept spiritual help. If this is you, take heart in learning that about half of the original AA members were in the same boat. They considered themselves atheists or agnostics, and they didn't believe in any sort of God. But after giving AA's solution a try and discovering God could save them from the drink, they came to believe.

Wherever you fall on the spectrum of faith, this chapter can help you understand the spiritual aspect of AA's approach to recovery.

A Solution or a Crutch?

One of the program's premises is that we must find a spiritual basis for our lives. The authors remind us that our moral codes and life philosophies didn't give us any type of control. We had lost control. We had lost power. On our own, we couldn't stop using. Eventually, we realized that if we wanted to quit and stay quit, we had to find a Power greater than ourselves.

That's the AA definition of God: a Power greater than ourselves. We admit we lack the power necessary to stop our addiction. We admit we are not God. Then, we seek a Power greater than ourselves that can help us quit. This is the beginning of a spiritual approach to life. The Big Book serves as a guide to get us started on the solution.

Still, many of us faced barriers. Perhaps we had honest doubts. Or we had discarded childhood images of God that had outlived their usefulness. Or we had dismissed God as a crutch for those who are weak or stupid. Or we rebelled against whatever we'd been taught. Whatever the reason, any mention of God made us defensive. Nope, not for me.

> Beware of that impulse to instantly reject God. It can keep us from having what we want: relief from our addiction. Ask yourself if you've given the spiritual life a fair chance—not on your terms, but on its own terms. Find out for yourself and from your own experience who and what this Higher Power might be.

We knew from the way drugs and alcohol roughed us up that we had to find another way. Beaten, many of us were open at least to examine what AA suggested. Freed from others' definition of God, we can develop our own concept of God.

The simple willingness to believe in a Power greater than ourselves is enough to start. That willingness opens us up to discovery.

Many people focus on nature when seeking a Power greater than themselves. Gazing upon a mountain ridge or across the ocean or up at the stars helps us feel part of something much bigger than us. Even in marveling at small details—a pinecone, a robin's egg, an agate—we gain a sense of awe. These can be stirrings of faith in a Power greater than ourselves.

God only knows where these stirrings will lead. There are all sorts of conceptions of God—as many as there are members in AA. Yet they seem to agree on one belief: a Power greater than themselves has accomplished the miraculous—what for them was not humanly possible. A Higher Power allowed them to quit drinking and drugging, empowering them to change their way of thinking and living. A Higher Power can bring us peace, happiness, and a sense of purpose. Millions of people worldwide have discovered this for themselves.

Seeing through New Eyes

The change required in our thinking and living is nothing short of radical. We need to see the world through new eyes. The Big Book talks about how people laughed at Christopher Columbus. "Don't sail too far, you'll fall off the earth," they cautioned. You know the rest of the story. He forced them to see the world in a new way.

Likewise, our drinking and drugging has forced us to find a new way to look at life. If we don't want to stay on the destructive path of addiction, we need to try a new path. Our ideas hadn't worked for us. The God idea had worked for others.

For all of the facts only a mouse click away, no one has a complete understanding of God. No one has cornered the market on truth. Beware those who tell you they have! God remains a mystery.

We still must search within ourselves to explore that mystery. It can help to listen to other people's journeys. Many of the personal stories in the Big Book can guide our own exploration. We can learn from the struggles, fumblings, and discoveries of fellow pilgrims and apply what they've learned to our own journey.

As we open our hearts and our ears (remember how

addiction had closed them up?), we may discover some surprises about ourselves. For instance, we might be surprised to realize we were a people of faith, even if we placed our faith squarely upon our own thinking. We might also realize that worship was already a part of our lives, though maybe what we worshipped—drugs, for example—only hurt us. Further, we might discover we were believers, even if it was simply in the existence of life itself. The spiritual life might not be such a stretch for us, after all.

The Big Book says that each of us, deep down, has a basic idea of God. This is common among all people in all cultures. Humans have tried to understand God since the beginning of time. Just as we need friends, the Big Book tells us we need faith in a Higher Power.

No Thunder, No Lightning

In chapter 4 we meet a minister's son, an atheist who is lying in a hospital bed. Suddenly he realizes, *Who am I to say there is no God?* After all, his drinking had brought him to his knees. He felt an immediate conviction and God's presence. That set him on the road to recovery. He never drank again.

Most spiritual experiences aren't that dramatic. They happen without lightning bolts, without thunderclaps. They occur slowly and subtly. Gradually, we come to believe. Gradually, we change our way of thinking and living. Gradually, we accept that God has done for us what we couldn't do for ourselves. Gradually, we become a miracle of recovery.

The Big Book suggests that the fundamental belief in God resides in you as well. All you have to do is be willing and open to the idea and you'll likely become aware of your faith. You'll discover your concept of God.

5

HOW IT WORKS

Resentment is like taking poison in
hopes your enemy will die.

Chapter 5 is the Big Book's most famous chapter. Its first two
and a half pages are read at most AA meetings. That opening
line—"Rarely have we seen a person fail who has thoroughly
followed our path"—has become as familiar to AA members
as "Fourscore and seven years ago . . ." But don't confuse fa-
miliarity with comprehension.

This chapter describes the guts of the program. Chapter 5
introduces the Twelve Steps, with special emphasis on Steps
Three and Four. Steps Three and Four move us from relying
on ourselves to relying on a Higher Power. Ultimately, these
Steps point us toward what we all want: a life of sobriety.

Notice the emphasis placed on honesty in the first page
alone. Who fails? Those who can't be honest with themselves.
What's required to get and stay clean and sober? The capacity
to be honest. Willingness to go to any length. Living in a way
that demands total honesty.

If you've read this far, you've probably decided that you
want to be freed from your addiction. Okay, but if you want

what recovering people have, the Big Book says, you must be willing to go to any length to get it. You must be willing to be fearless and thorough in your honesty. That's what is necessary for you to take the steps that lead to the solution.

Not surprisingly, some hesitate. It seems natural for the addict to want to find "an easier, softer way." Some look for the shortcut, but that won't do. The old ideas have got to go. No other way works.

Spiritual Crossroads

You stand at a crossroads. Which path will you choose? Will you continue along the road of destruction, or will you accept the spiritual solution?

If you decide that you want sobriety, then you're ready to take certain steps. Note that the Twelve Steps are *suggested* as a program of recovery. Nobody is forcing you to do this, so you don't need to rebel. You can put away that knee-jerk reflex to refuse. The authors—speaking for thousands of AA members—are simply saying, "Here's what we did; it worked for us; why don't you try it? These are the Steps we suggest you take."

Each of the Steps deserves considerable study. We'll do that in this and the following chapters. For now, it's enough just to get to know them, which can be a bit intimidating at first.

The first time I read the Twelve Steps, I wanted to give up. I said, "Are you serious? *This* is what I've got to do to get clean and sober? No way." Who, upon first seeing these Steps, thinks, *No problem?* Nobody.

The Big Book's authors anticipated our reaction. They tell us that no one can work the Steps perfectly. Well, that's a relief. I don't have to be perfect to make it. They aren't, and they did it.

They're not saints. So, I don't have to be a spiritual Superman. That takes a load off. I simply must be willing to grow spiritually. That's easy enough. To strive for progress rather than perfection also seems within my reach. Immediately after listing the Steps, the authors reassure us that they're do-able.

Following that, the chapter summarizes the ABCs of the first two Steps: we had lost control; we couldn't relieve our addiction on our own; we needed God's help. If we truly believed that, we were ready for Step Three.

Step Three: Made a decision to turn our will and our lives over to the care of God *as we understood Him.*

This calls for some of that rigorous honesty talked about earlier. We're asked to admit our selfishness—not easy for anyone. Yet our self-centeredness has been the root of our troubles. Even when we thought others were to blame for our problems, if we looked closely, we'd see that our problems usually started with us. It's not enough to cork the bottle, snuff the pipe, or flush the pills. We've got to admit and abandon our selfish ways.

We must rid ourselves of this selfishness or it'll kill us. It's that serious. Selfishness usually leads to relapse. And relapse, in our case, is often fatal. Now, we can't rely on ourselves to be rid of our self-centeredness—it would be rather self-centered to think we could, don't you think? There's help. God can deliver us from our self-centeredness.

That's where Step Three comes in. We turn our will and our lives over to the care of God. (And, remember, this is the God of your conception, no one else's.) The Big Book suggests a prayer, but it's easy to get hung up on the "thees" and "thous" here. To many of us, this prayer comes across a bit churchy and outdated. Maybe you can try something like this instead: "God, I offer myself to you. Shape me and guide me. Relieve me of my selfishness so that I may better do your will. Take away my troubles so that others may see the love and power you're capable of. Help me always to do your will."

Whatever words you use, the idea is to turn over your will and life to the care of God, however you can best express that. You might simply say, "God, I turn my thoughts and my actions over to your care."

For me, it helped to know that I wasn't submitting myself to an uncaring or indifferent, spiteful God. I tried to remember I was surrendering my will and life to the *care* of a loving God. To a God who wants what's best for me. To a God who can run things a lot smoother than I did, despite my delusions otherwise.

Relatively early in my recovery, a young woman helped me understand how my will and God's will came together. She said that she believed her deepest desires—to be loved, to belong, to feel a sense of purpose—were also God's deepest desires for her. She admitted that she often became distracted by superficial and selfish wants but, deep down, her will matched God's will.

That thought has helped me enormously in working the Third Step. It seems the Third Step is about getting honest with myself and my fundamental idea of God, which will, in turn, line up my will with God's.

Step Four: Made a searching and fearless moral inventory of ourselves.

With Step Three, we admitted our selfishness had caused many of our problems. With Step Four, we detail our part in those problems. In doing so, we admit that the alcohol and drugs were but symptoms; the root of our addiction lay in our selfish nature. We have met the enemy, and the enemy is us. Step Four requires us to look for the flaws that caused our failure. This lets us begin to make peace with the past and change the course of our future.

> The disease of addiction isn't only physical and mental, but spiritual as well. When we treat our spiritual illness, we regain our physical and mental health. We start by rooting out our resentments, which are the source of our spiritual illness.

Put It in Black and White

Resentment is anger that won't go away. It hardens within us like plaque in arteries and chokes off our supply of life-giving contact from our Higher Power. Others might be able to handle anger, but we can't. The risk to our spiritual health is too severe. Hanging on to anger not only will lead to frustration and unhappiness; it could kill us. Resentments lead to relapse. That, in turn, could be fatal. If we are to be free of our addiction, we must—with our Higher Power's help—let go of our resentments. The Fourth Step helps us begin that process.

The Big Book recommends taking a searching and fearless moral inventory by writing it out on paper. If you're more comfortable at the keyboard, type it on a computer. The important thing is that you commit your inventory to the written word.

Why? Several reasons. For starters, once we start writing, this creative process helps us think of more things to add. It also requires a certain honesty to commit our inventory to black and white—we can't fudge things on paper the way we can in our minds. Further, by listing our resentments, fears, and other flaws on paper, we place them outside of ourselves. This can be symbolic as we work to overcome our short-comings. Finally, it will be helpful to have this list when we take the Fifth Step.

The Big Book outlines a four-column approach to taking an inventory. Although page 65 lists only three columns, the instructions add a fourth column two pages later. Here's how it works:

- In the first column, we list our resentments toward people, institutions, or principles. Whatever made us angry, we make a separate entry for it.
- In the second column, we list what it was about that person, institution, or principle that made us angry. We are as specific as possible.
- In the third column, we list how that anger affected or injured us. We identify the area of our lives where we felt the impact.
- In the fourth column, we look for where we were to blame. Often our selfishness came into play. Here's where we need to be especially searching and fearless. We list our faults and wrongs with each situation.

No Defect Too Small

Once we've made it through our resentments, we continue with our fears in the same four-column manner. Then we move on to sex, listing where we've been selfish, dishonest, or inconsiderate. We list the people we've hurt and how we have been at fault. You can keep going with whatever else comes to mind. Money might trigger several entries. So, too, might authority figures if you haven't included them with your resentments. With each category, list everything you can think of. Go as far back in your memory as possible. No resentment or defect is too small to list. Be searching and fearless.

Next, take note of fear. This seems to invade every aspect of our lives. Self-reliance won't help us with fear. Self-sufficiency for us is an illusion that has turned into an obsession. The Third Step, however, helps us let go of that foolish thinking.

Turning our will and our lives over to the care of God, we transfer our reliance from ourselves to God. We place our trust in God. This puts us on the road to serenity, one of the benefits of sobriety.

Some might consider such trust in God to be a weakness. It's not.

In surrendering our will, we find a strength. That's the program's paradox (a statement that seems to contradict itself). Our power comes from the admission of our powerlessness. With God, we can do what we could not by ourselves. So, we ask God to remove our fear and shape us into who He (or She) would have us be.

About sex: One of the wonderful coincidences of the Big Book is that talk of sex takes place on page 69. With that noted, you're not likely to forget where to turn should you become troubled by sex-related issues.

No need to be alarmed by your sex problems—we've all got them; that makes us human. Recognizing that takes the shame out of them. Remember, we're not saints. The point is, that we're willing to grow along spiritual lines. So, too, in our sex lives.

With the Fourth Step, we're shaping "a sane and sound

ideal" for our future sexual activity. Our concept of sex resembles our concept of God: it's as we understand it from our experience. Here, as in every other aspect of our lives, we must get honest. The Big Book suggests a simple test for each sexual encounter: Is it selfish or not? If we discover it's selfish, we must reconsider our actions. If not and it's in line with our sane and sound ideal, green light.

Remember, we must be responsible for our sexuality. If we have problems, it's wise to turn to counselors and doctors for advice. When the Big Book was written sixty years ago, people didn't need to worry about HIV and AIDS, but other unwanted STDs did exist as did pregnancy and sexual assault.

We pray to God for help in modeling our ideal and the strength to follow it. Also, we remember that our sexuality is a gift from God, something to be treasured and respected. With the Third Step in mind, we trust God to guide us.

Some of us continue to struggle with sexual issues well into sobriety. Like alcohol and drugs, sex can be cunning, baffling, and powerful. Being careless with sex can lead to relapse. Again, if you have questions or unresolved issues related to sex, reach out to trustworthy people for advice.

Completing the inventory is the first part of cleaning up our past. At this point, you're off to a good start. You've shown the honesty that the Twelve Steps call for. The honesty necessary to maintain sobriety. The honesty necessary to work the solution. Good job.

6

INTO ACTION

Humility doesn't mean thinking any less of yourself;
it means thinking of yourself less often.

This is a program of action. The solution doesn't come knocking on our door; we have to work for it. Here's how. This chapter walks us through Steps 5 through 11. It shows us how to complete our housecleaning and make peace with the past. As with the first four Steps, this program of action requires honesty and humility. It also promises our efforts will be rewarded.

Step Five: Admitted to God, to ourselves, and to another human being the exact nature of our wrongs.

The Fifth Step is critical in our recovery. You may be tempted to skip this Step, but that could be a shortcut back to addiction. Over the years, I've noticed that repeat relapsers have something in common: they didn't complete Step Five. Don't let that be you.

This Step demands rigorous honesty—with God, ourselves, and another person. You may want to leave others out of it, but admitting our wrongs to another person helps us get honest with ourselves. The Fifth Step requires us to be humble, fearless, and honest. This is a proven way to get clean and stay clean. It also is the secret to a happy life.

While using, many of us were two-faced. There was the face we wanted others to see and the face we wanted to hide. We lived in fear that others would discover who we really were—then ridicule and reject us. We turned to our addiction for relief from this fear and tension. Stepping forward and telling someone else all that we've hidden away reduces our shame. It relieves the fear and tension. We no longer have to worry about somebody finding out—we've already told someone. And, miracle of miracles, we discover it doesn't kill us to tell.

Be careful when choosing someone to hear your Fifth Step. Pick someone you can trust to keep your story confidential. That might be a minister, priest, or rabbi, but it doesn't have to be. It could be your sponsor or counselor. Choose someone who approves of what you're trying to do in coming clean. Choose someone who's willing to listen without judging. Finally, choose someone who has a certain emotional distance and isn't affected personally by what you reveal.

Once you've found that special someone to hear your Fifth Step, do it. Don't delay. The time to get clean and sober is now. Don't put your recovery on hold.

Most people dread going into their Fifth Step. Yet, upon completion—having admitted everything and withheld nothing—the Big Book promises positive results.

We'll discover a sense of peace and relief. Our fears will disappear. We'll feel the presence of a Higher Power. We may even feel that our addiction has lifted. This is the beginning of a spiritual experience.

After finishing your Fifth Step, the Big Book suggests this:

- Find a place where you can be quiet for an hour.
- There, thank God sincerely for getting to know Him or Her better.
- Review the first five Steps and ask yourself if there's anything you've left out.
- If you're satisfied with how you've done, then you're ready to move on to Steps Six and Seven, which can also be completed in this hour.

Step Six: Were entirely ready to have God remove all these defects of character.

In identifying what's wrong with us, many of us are ready to say, "Take it away, God." Yet, there may be some defects, perhaps our pride or certain fears, that we have trouble releasing. With these, we ask God for the willingness to let go of them. Mostly, the process of going through the first five Steps has made us ready.

There's a difference between being ready and being willing. Consider two people standing at the start of a marathon. One is willing to run the race. The other is willing *and ready*, having done months of training. Which runner do you expect to cross the finish line? The first five Steps have been our training for the Sixth and Seventh Steps. It's not recommended to attempt Step Six without first doing Four and Five. Don't try Step Six before you're ready.

Step Seven: Humbly asked Him to remove our shortcomings.

That brings us to Step Seven, the follow-up to Six. With humility, recognizing that we haven't been able to do this for ourselves, we ask God to remove our shortcomings. It's the final release of all the baggage you exposed. You don't have to carry that anymore. You can let go of it.

The Big Book offers a prayer, sometimes called the Seventh Step prayer. You can use these words or find your own. Basically, the idea is to say something like, "Here I am, God. This is me, good and bad, as you've seen in my inventory. Please remove my shortcomings so that I may be useful to you and others. Give me the strength necessary to do your will."

Yes, it's humbling to turn our will over to God. It's humbling to desire to be useful to others. But this humility is the medicine for our "self-will run riot." It cures our ego. Not in a way that demeans or diminishes us. On the contrary, this humility reminds us that we're another child of God—neither better nor worse than others—fully deserving of divine love.

Step Eight: Made a list of all persons we had harmed, and became willing to make amends to them all.

We started this list with Step Four. Now we review it and add anyone who might be missing. First, we make sure we've listed all of the people we've harmed. Then we become willing to make amends.

When making our list, we don't consider whether or not we feel like making amends to certain people. We'll be willing to approach some of these folks right away. Not so with others. They're the ones we would want to avoid—or punch in the face—if we spotted them in the lobby of a movie theater. We're reluctant to add them to the list. But we do so, and we pray for the willingness to make amends. We also pray for the grace to be able to forgive those who have harmed us.

This takes further humility. It doesn't mean we humiliate ourselves—place ourselves beneath others. Rather, it means we humble ourselves—we don't place ourselves above others. Humility helps us develop an honest understanding of our relationship to others.

One AA saying describes the alcoholic as "an ego maniac with an inferiority complex." Constantly feeling less than others, we fought to prove ourselves better. Humility frees us from that obsession. We see that we're all children of God, who doesn't play favorites.

Step Nine: Made direct amends to such people wherever possible, except when to do so would injure them or others.

In working Steps Four through Nine, we clean up our past and make things right with others by repairing the damage we've done. The Big Book reminds us that these actions pave the way for us to be of service to God and other people.

The reminder is well placed. We can't just clean house, then trash the place again. The secret to maintaining sobriety and living a purposeful life lies in serving others. We work these Steps to make us fit for such service.

Notice that we made *direct* amends. To face our past, we must face others. When it's not practical or possible to make an amend in person—perhaps because of distance between us—we make a phone call, write a letter, or send an e-mail. We try to be as direct as possible.

Remember, actions speak louder than words. To amend something means to change it. We change our behavior. We stop doing whatever it was that harmed others. To take it a step further, we can try to show kindness toward them. If this seems too extreme in certain cases, we can start by praying for the other person's well-being. Often such prayer is enough to soften our feelings toward another.

Always, we keep the focus on us. Regardless of what the other person may have done, we're there to clean our side of the street. We're working off our inventory, not anyone else's. He or she has to live in his or her mess; we no longer want to live in ours.

Sometimes—often, even—we get wonderful results once we apologize, but that's not always the case. It can't be our expectation. It's not why we make amends. We work Step Nine so we may be free of our past and enjoy a future without addiction. This Step is an important brick in the arch through which we will walk a free person.

The Big Book talks about amends around money, a touchy subject for most of us. These amends may make us want to hide, but we can't. We must work these Steps in all areas of our lives, not just those where it's convenient or easy. Remember, *half-measures availed us nothing*. To build that arch, we must practice rigorous honesty. If we try to hide from those we owe money, that fear and dishonesty could be the trap door through which we fall back into our addiction. We must face them and work out a realistic plan to pay off our debts.

There may be serious consequences to our honesty. We may end up paying money we wouldn't have had to if we had kept our mouth shut. We may face jail time if we admit an offense. We could get suspended from school for fessing up to a wrong. No matter. Here again, we must practice rigorous honesty.

Don't Hurt Others

Without this honesty, we'll remain afraid of our past. And when our past still has its grip on us, we're not yet free of our addiction. Once again, we must choose between our addiction and freedom. We must go at this solution whole-heartedly. There are no shortcuts. How bad do you want to be clean and sober?

Now let's talk about this phrase in Step Nine: *Except when to do so would injure them or others*. What does this mean? Keep in mind that we're trying to become more useful to others. We don't want to do something that would hurt others. Sometimes admitting past actions will harm others unnecessarily. For example, say you cheated on your boyfriend or girlfriend. Naming the person you fooled around with would unnecessarily harm that person. Let him or her remain anonymous.

Or, say you're confessing to a crime that you committed with another. You need not confess for the other person as well. Leave him or her out of it. Or, perhaps there's something you did that your parents don't know about and that didn't affect them directly. Telling them would hurt them. Don't tell them. In such cases, we become willing to make amends but don't actually go through with them in order to spare others further harm. The Big Book provides examples of praying for help and finding creative means of making amends. Try this if you find yourself stuck.

Sobriety Isn't Enough

Although we must stop using, doing so is not by itself a sufficient amend. In other words, sobriety isn't enough. It's great you quit using, but repairing the damage can take years.

The Big Book recommends we sit down with our family to

begin this reconstruction. Careful to keep the focus on ourselves, we examine the past and how we might set things right. We don't take an inventory of our family members. Nor do we criticize them, regardless of what their faults and actions may have been.

This will be difficult. Remember, the solution is simple, not easy. Remember, too, there is help. We pray for patience, tolerance, kindness, and love. We pray for this daily, hourly when necessary. In this way, we seek peace at home.

Be careful, too, not to impose your new views on others. Many of us get swept away by our own spiritual experience. We want to share the good news with others. This, however, isn't always respectful of what they've been through. It's better to hold back. Our place is not to preach.

The Big Book tells us we have to live the spiritual life. This is a program of action, not relaxation. Nothing comes to the passive observer. To receive the benefits of these spiritual principles, we must apply them to our lives.

The authors then make several promises. They say if we're thorough and painstaking in working the Steps, by the end of Step Nine our lives will have changed. We'll feel better about ourselves. Action brings results. Not everyone is on the same timetable, but the authors promise us if we do the work, we'll get results.

Step Ten: Continued to take personal inventory and when we were wrong promptly admitted it.

Steps One through Nine clean up our past. Steps Ten through Twelve maintain our sobriety in the present.

Note that Step Ten says "when" not "if" we were wrong. We will be wrong again. We will stumble. Our faults will trip us up. *No one can perfectly follow these principles.* When we're wrong, we try to set things right "promptly." Watch out for selfishness, dishonesty, resentment, and fear. They're certain to trip you up. When they do, ask God again to remove these shortcomings.

The Big Book also promises that the obsession to use will slip away. You may still occasionally have using dreams or occasional twinges to use. But as we practice the program of action, the overwhelming desire to get wasted tends to fade. That, however, isn't a sign that we can take it easy and stop working on our recovery.

There's no place for spiritual couch potatoes in this program of action. That can lead to relapse. So long as we stay spiritually fit, we'll stay sober another day.

Step Eleven: Sought through prayer and meditation to improve our conscious contact with God *as we understood Him*, praying only for knowledge of His will for us and the power to carry that out.

Notice how the Steps refer to God as "Him" and "His." Some people would rather not give God a male identity. Feel free to substitute words that fit your understanding. This is the God of your conception we're talking about, whoever She—or He—may be.

The Big Book suggests that we do an inventory at the end of the day. This can be done anytime in your daily routine—on the bus or subway, in your morning prayer, while flossing, whenever. The key is to make it a daily habit like brushing your teeth. The Big Book offers questions to help you be honest and thorough in this inventory. Recall when God was present in your interactions and active in your life over the past twenty-four hours, and then express your gratitude.

The Big Book also suggests that we start each day by asking God for direction, inspiration, and freedom from self-will. Throughout the day, we pause, especially when upset or confused, and ask again for direction and inspiration. It's useful to repeat an abbreviated version of the Third Step prayer, "Your will be done." Over time, we learn to trust ourselves as we see that God is working within us. That's when we know we're living God's will and not our own.

7

WORKING WITH OTHERS

I need all the help I can give.

This chapter focuses on Step Twelve: "Having had a spiritual awakening as the result of these steps, we tried to carry this message to alcoholics, and to practice these principles in all our affairs."

The Step assumes that after working the first eleven Steps, we have had some sort of spiritual experience. This could range from a profound event to the simple willingness to work these Steps. At the very least, we've started to see our limitations. We've become willing to put some belief in a Power greater than ourselves. We've also become aware of God doing for us what we couldn't do for ourselves. These are spiritual experiences.

Step Twelve tells us to practice these spiritual principles in all areas of our lives. They're not just to get us out of trouble. We try to be rigorously honest in everything we do. We try to be patient, kind, and tolerant with everyone we meet. We aim to be helpful in all situations. We pray for God's guidance and inspiration in whatever we do. In short, we practice these principles in *all* our affairs.

Step Twelve talks about carrying the message. We each have something unique to offer others. Our addiction gives us a special understanding of other addicts. Our experience can give others hope. It can even offer them new life. Our past, no matter how far down we had fallen, can save others' lives.

That adds meaning to our own lives. Our past allows us to connect with others and to develop relationships built on a deep and secure bond. It also lets us reach out to those still in need of help. That gives us a purpose.

The Big Book suggests where you might find others to help. You might also find them in your school, neighborhood, dorm, church, temple, or clubs. You can offer your services to other "helping professionals," such as rabbis, priests, pastors, guidance counselors, and doctors. Tell them you're willing to talk to other young people who may be addicts. Be careful not to criticize their efforts to help. You can simply tell them that carrying the message to others is a big part of your own recovery program.

Alcoholics Anonymous (AA) meetings are another place for you to connect with other young people. Introduce yourself to newcomers and offer to talk with them.

Because you have gotten clean and sober, you have something special to offer other young people. You can be especially helpful to other young people like yourself—whether you're female, male, Native American, African American, Asian American, gay or lesbian, and so on. This doesn't mean people of similar backgrounds can always relate to each other or that those who are quite different won't be able to help each other. As fellow addicts, we all have much in common. It's just that the closer your experience is to that of another person, the more you may be able to understand one another on issues outside of your addiction. This can be especially helpful at first.

Early in recovery, many of us sailed along on a "pink cloud" after we found these Steps working for us. But beware. Don't put yourself on a mission to convert others. Yes, we become excited about the good things this program has done for us, but it's easy to get carried away and lose sight of how we might appear to others.

If someone tried to cram this program down your throat you would no doubt gag too. Consider how you might want others to talk to you. What worked for you? Try that with others. A calm, reasoned approach is easier to swallow. If you find yourself on a mission, mellow out.

These guidelines can help in talking to others about their drug or alcohol use:

- Don't talk to them if they're drunk or high. They won't be able to hear what you have to say.
- If possible, talk to them after their use has gotten them into trouble. They may be more open to your message.
- Talk to them in person. Being able to see one another will build trust and help you "read" how they're responding to you.
- Meet with them alone. This gives you more freedom to talk without pressure from parents or others.

The Big Book suggests a blueprint for your first meeting with someone seeking help. The following suggestions can also help:

- Find common ground.
- Talk about the illness.
- Talk about the solution.
- Know when to go.

Find Common Ground

For starters, before you talk about your drinking and drugging, see if you can find some common interest to connect you. This might include music, sports, movies, or hobbies. Ease into talk of your use. Mention how drinking and drugging caused you problems. Make the connection between your use and your consequences. For example, "I got arrested for DWI, not because the cop was out to get me as I originally accused him, but because I was driving while drunk. My drinking cost me my license, which in turn cost me my job."

If they want to talk, let them. It's great if the other person is willing to open up about how drinking and drugging turned on him or her. Let the person give a few personal examples.

Once you've established this connection, tell him or her how you came to understand that you were an alcoholic or addict. Explain how you learned that alcohol and/or drugs caused your problems. Explain how you admitted you had lost control—that once you started using, you couldn't control the amount you used to stop the consequences from coming. Add how you resisted believing this at first, and mention your obsession to control and enjoy your use.

If the person you're talking to is an addict, he or she will relate. You don't have to make a diagnosis. Even though it may be obvious to you that the person is an addict, he or she must come to this understanding and admission himself or herself, just as you did. You can't take the First Step for anyone else. You can only show the way to it.

Talk about the Illness

It might help others to learn that addiction is an illness. They didn't get where they are because they're bad people. If they are addicts, they're sick. You can explain that addiction is a disease that's usually inherited, just like cancer or heart disease. Their addiction was a disease just waiting to happen. It's like a pilot light in a furnace. Once they took that first drink or hit—voomp! the flame flared up full force.

To demonstrate that addiction is now officially considered a disease, mention that medical doctors look for specific symptoms in diagnosing alcoholism and chemical dependency. They are outlined in the *DSM-IV (Diagnostic and Statistical Manual of Mental Disorders)*, published by the American Psychiatric Association. This is a physician's bible.

Here are some of the symptoms listed for both alcoholism and chemical dependency:

- tolerance (increased drinking to achieve the same effect)
- withdrawal signs or symptoms
- consumption in larger amounts than intended
- unsuccessful attempts to cut down on use
- excessive time related to alcohol or drugs (obtaining, hangover, and so on)
- impaired social or work activities due to use

- continued use despite bad consequences in the following areas: social, occupational, psychological, and physical

Finally, you might add that we believe addiction is a terminal illness, one that ends in insanity and death if left untreated.

Talk about the Solution

The authors instruct you to wait for the person to ask how you got well. This is beautiful, the way they've laid out this approach in the Big Book. You've told the other person how you were sick, and now he or she is identifying, "Yes, me too, sounds a lot like what happened to me." You've described your seemingly hopeless condition and the twisted thinking that went along with it, yet you're sitting there obviously sober and living a fulfilled life. No doubt the person will be curious how you got from there (what you're describing) to here (how you are today). He or she will want to know how to make such a change too. Once you're asked, tell the truth.

As you discuss the spiritual side of the program, remember that this person doesn't have to believe in your concept of God, no matter how convinced you may be of it. Emphasize this point: What's required is willingness to believe in a Power greater than oneself and to live by spiritual principles. You might describe how you were turned off by this idea at first and what won you over.

Be careful not to criticize whatever beliefs he or she may have. You can mention how you learned that faith alone won't save the addict from himself or herself and addiction. Faith must be accompanied by works. This is a program of action. *The spiritual life isn't a theory—we have to live it.* Explain that we've found a solution that requires a plan of action.

Outline the Twelve Steps suggested as a program of recovery. Mention the Twelfth Step is what you're doing right now by meeting with him or her. Explain that carrying the message keeps you sober. Most of us have never failed on a Twelfth Step call. Regardless of whether the other person quit using, we didn't use while we were speaking with him or her. Thank the person for allowing you to work your program and stay clean and sober.

Be careful not to say, "You *should* do this" or "You *shouldn't* do that." That's likely to trigger a defensive or rebellious reaction. AA doesn't have any hard or fast rules, only suggestions based on what has worked for others. You can explain this and add that there's no pressure or obligation whatsoever. If the person seems interested in AA, give him or her a copy of the Big Book to read. He or she can make the choice to persist in addiction, try to fix it on his or her own, or check out our way. Leave the other person free to choose.

Know When to Go

So you've described your experience—what it was like, what happened, and how the program helped. You've answered the person's questions. Make sure he or she knows how to contact you or find a meeting. Say good-bye. You may or may not hear from the person. He or she may be ready to quit or may need to experience more consequences before becoming ready to try our solution. The person may never be ready. That's God's affair. We've done what we can to this point. The rest we turn over to God.

Look for your next prospect. You can't sit at home waiting for the first person to call for further help. We must keep active ourselves and continue to work our program of action.

If a person does call after your first visit and express interest in learning more, offer practical advice on working the Twelve Steps. He or she may ask for additional help, financial or otherwise. The Big Book suggests that we provide what's within our means but not what's beyond them. We are to be generous, especially with our time, to put as much energy into our recovery as we did into our use. Think about how much time and effort you put into scoring a fix, getting high or drunk, and nursing hangovers. That's what it took for us to descend into our addiction; it will require at least that much time and effort to ascend into our recovery. That time and effort is well spent on Twelfth Step work.

Set Boundaries

In helping others, we need to set boundaries. Don't deprive yourself of necessities, such as food or shelter. Don't endanger yourself or others. If you offer someone money, set a limit and stick to it. For instance, tell the person that you'll provide twenty dollars, no more. This protects you from getting milked and lets the person know you will not take care of his or her responsibilities.

Keep the emphasis on what you are able to offer spiritually. Here, give freely and abundantly. Those who are truly ready to recover will find you meeting their primary need. Some may blame you for not helping them enough. Just remember: still-suffering addicts or alcoholics need to trust in God. Then they need to clean their own house. That's what worked for you. It should be good enough for them.

Chapter 7 talks about marriage and divorce. This advice can also be applied to those of us who still live at home. We're told to focus on ourselves. We're to clean our side of the street, leaving our parents' and other family members' inventories to themselves. Our goal is to be sober, considerate, and helpful, regardless of how others behave.

Your efforts to help others may lead to daily contact. They may lean on you day to day. This will bring rewards to both of you. When we put ourselves in God's hands, life is better than anything we could have planned. Newcomers to the program will also discover this.

A Few Warnings

Chapter 7 says to beware of getting involved in the person's family arguments. Avoid taking sides. If the person's family members approach you, remind them that God is at work in the individual and encourage them to trust in that. The individual's problems didn't happen overnight; they won't go away overnight.

The Big Book offers a sane guideline about staying out of harm's way. It's best to avoid places where there is drinking and drugging. Visiting an old—or new—using haunt simply to test ourselves is probably not a good idea. Going there to eat a meal or to pick up someone who needs help or to attend a birthday party, for example, may be okay. If we can honestly tell ourselves and God that our reason for going there is legitimate, then we'll probably be okay. If we're working our program, we'll be in good shape. Another good suggestion: If you have any doubts about going somewhere, bring another recovering person along for support. You can help keep each other honest and sober.

This advice reminds us that we don't have to be hermits, withdrawn from the world. It's okay to get out and participate in life. It's good for our recovery to enjoy ourselves among others. With time, we find we can do so without problems.

Another comment on balancing our approach to life: Our

desire to help the alcoholic or addict who still suffers is not a crusade to ban alcohol or other drugs. Alcohol and drugs aren't the problem, addiction is. That's what we focus on— the problem of addiction. We work to help ourselves by helping the addict who still suffers.

The authors of the Big Book hoped that the public would eventually understand alcoholism. Sixty years later, that seems to have come to pass. This is probably due to how we recovering people have worked the program. If we keep sharing our experience, strength, and hope one at a time with others still suffering, we'll likely make more progress over the next sixty years. The need will still be there. Though we'll make progress, the problem will probably never go away.

8

TO WIVES

Codependency: You're drowning and someone
else's life flashes before your eyes.

To wives? I didn't even have a date for the homecoming dance.
What's this wives stuff got to do with your recovery?

The chapter begins by explaining that although the authors
have been speaking about men, their message also applies to
women. I might add that it holds true for others who don't
readily see themselves in the examples. Addiction is an equal
opportunity disease. It doesn't discriminate based on gender,
race, age, sexual orientation, or religion. Fortunately, Alcoholics Anonymous is an equal opportunity program. Its solution is available to all alcoholics and addicts—provided, of
course, that they can be honest.

The Big Book was written with men in mind, and many
of those men in the early AA program had wives. This chapter was written for them. But its message goes well beyond
wives—and is also recommended reading for the addict.
Chapter 8 talks about how addiction affects those we love.
When you see addiction through the eyes of your loved ones,
you see how your addiction impacted them. You also see

where they'll struggle with their own recovery and how you can be supportive.

Share this chapter with those who love you. Ask them to read it. These concerned persons include your parents, sisters, brothers, girlfriends, boyfriends, close friends, perhaps grandparents, aunts and uncles, even wives and husbands, if that fits. This chapter speaks directly to them. So, too, will I.

To Family Members and Friends

In this chapter, you, the concerned person, will learn about the disease we face. For a more complete understanding, I encourage you to read the entire Big Book, especially its first eleven chapters, but chapter 8 is a good beginning. In it you'll come to see how this disease is a family disease and has impacted you. You'll also see how the solution involves you—regardless of the addict's progress with recovery—and how you can work your own program of recovery. In this chapter, you'll find hope.

Chapter 8 is written by wives to wives, but you don't need to be a wife to benefit from the authors' advice. If you love someone with an alcohol or drug problem, you'll quickly relate to what they have to say. The chapter is built upon the same premise of Alcoholics Anonymous: Those who have been there themselves understand what you're going through. Our experience provides a special understanding and bond.

Here, too, it doesn't matter if you're the wife of an alcoholic or the father of a teenage crankhead. Your common experience of loving someone who can't quit by himself or herself helps you understand each other's fears and frustrations. If it helps as you're reading, you can replace "husbands" with "sons," "daughters," or whatever fits your situation.

Right off, the chapter lays out the problem for concerned

persons. It details how the disease may have affected your life. If you find yourself nodding along with the description of pride, frustration, self-pity, misunderstanding, fear, anger, and resentment, then you realize these women know what they're talking about. You can relate to the internal conflict between the crazy hope that the addict will quit and the intense fear of the next outburst. You probably have your own examples of how, after you bailed the addict out of trouble, this person still blamed you for his or her problems.

You understand the pain of watching a loved one suffer remorse, depression, and inferiority. You know the sadness that comes upon realizing that despite all of your efforts, the addict still can't quit. You empathize with the baffling and heartbreaking aspect of the disease.

You've probably tried to control the addict's use in a number of ways, but you couldn't. Your efforts only made you feel angry, frustrated, and crazy. Perhaps you're even ready to admit that the addict's use made your life unmanageable and that you're powerless over whether he or she uses or quits. This is the first step in your own recovery.

It helps to understand that alcoholism and addiction are diseases, not moral failures or personal shortcomings. This doesn't excuse the behavior that goes along with the disease. Nor does it excuse the pain and suffering the addict causes others. But it does help explain why addicts do what they do. Why they keep using despite how it hurts them and others. They're sick.

Just as the alcoholic is sick, so, too, is the concerned person. This is a family disease. It's contagious among those the addict loves. Earlier, the Big Book describes the alcoholic as a tornado roaring through the lives of others. The tornado sweeps up the addict's loved ones and throws them into a crazy tilt. Yet, once again, it's through no moral failing or personal shortcoming on the concerned person's part. Though this doesn't excuse the concerned person's behavior, it does help explain it. Ultimately, the concerned person—like the addict—needs help.

"But I'm Not the Problem"

Perhaps you find this idea difficult to accept. You weren't the one out getting wasted and into trouble. Perhaps you're saying, "No, I'm not the problem. They are. Their use has caused our problems. If they would quit using, everything would be okay." But it's not that easy. Addiction twists everyone's thinking and distorts everyone's behavior. That's true of the addict, and that's true of the concerned person. The Big Book points out that the concerned person also carries the burdens of pride, self-pity, and vanity. Take away the drug of choice, and you've still got the twisted thinking and distorted behavior. This program of recovery addresses those—for both the addict and the concerned person. It promises a better way of life if you're willing to apply the spiritual principles laid out for the alcoholic. Al-Anon—the companion program to AA—makes this easier by modifying the Steps to meet your needs.

Whether the addicts are still using or are in recovery, concerned persons learn that they must change too. Just because the addicts may have changed doesn't mean *we* have. Their disease affected us, but their solution won't cure us; *we* won't get well by association. We must work our own program.

The Big Book outlines the progression of this illness by describing four categories of drinkers. The descriptions and the correlating suggestions build upon each other. It's a good idea to read through all of them.

You'll quickly see that this chapter isn't a set of instructions to get the addict to quit using. While it does offer some suggestions on how you might help, it focuses on how you can find a spiritual solution for yourself. The authors describe an emotional independence, where your moods are not dependent upon the addict's. You can be peaceful even if the alcoholic is angry. You can be happy when he or she is sad. Similarly, your relationships need not be determined by this person's behavior.

You don't have to wait for the addict to quit using to get on with your life. Though baffled and heartbroken, you can live. The same paradox applies to you as it does to the addict: Admitting your powerlessness gives you power. You'll find freedom by surrendering.

The Big Book points out that the one you love may suffer from problems greater than addiction, such as clinical depression or other mental illnesses. In these cases, it's wise to seek professional help.

No More Excuses

Another paradox applies to helping addicts: You can help them by letting them feel the pain of their disease. Stop making excuses for them. Let them be accountable for their own behavior and suffer the consequences of their use. If you protect them from the consequences, they won't feel them. They also won't feel motivated to change. When you stop enabling their use by protecting them from its consequences, you're demonstrating your love. In this way, you'll also be taking a giant stride toward your own emotional independence.

You may be reluctant to take this step. Probably, you worry

about consequences that threaten their personal well-being. In such situations, you can influence but not control things completely. For instance, if you suspect your daughter will be partying on a Friday night and you don't want her driving, don't give her the car keys.

Or, take the example of the husband and father losing his job. On the surface it isn't what anyone would wish, but it could turn out to be a blessing. It could be the consequence that brings the addict to his or her knees. If you try to protect addicts from that consequence, you could prevent them from hitting their knees.

In getting on with your own life, you're observing this motto: *Live and let live.* You become willing to embrace an attitude of patience, tolerance, understanding, and love. Your focus shifts from the addict to yourself. You look to what you can contribute to life rather than what you can take out of it. The Big Book promises that this change of thinking will make your life fuller and more peaceful.

Once you start applying these spiritual principles to your life and feeling the changes taking place, you'll find that you have a gift to offer others. You can reach out to help other concerned persons. You can provide understanding and wisdom from your own experience. Be careful, however, not to try to change them. You may be tempted to transfer your desire to fix the addict you love to another concerned person, but that's just a setup for another failure. Respect where others are, and remember what worked with you. Easy does it.

It's a good idea to learn more about codependency, a condition that often affects those who love an addict. Since the Big Book was written, a lot more has been written about how addiction impacts a family. You can find books on the subject at your local library or most bookstores.

The Al-Anon program can also be a source of understanding, support, education, and growth. As the footnote at the end of this chapter in the Big Book explains, chapter 8 was written before Al-Anon was formed. This companion program was designed to help the addict's loved ones and other concerned persons. It approaches alcoholism from their perspective, tailoring the Steps to their situation. Contact Al-Anon in your area to learn more. In this group, you'll find others who have been there. They'll be able to offer you—and you'll, in turn, be able to offer others—a special understanding.

9

THE FAMILY AFTERWARD

Laughter is the language of angels.

Chapter 9 is for addicts and family members. Because addiction is a family disease, the whole family needs healing. All will not be well if the addict simply quits using. There's a long road ahead for the whole family's recovery. This chapter provides directions to get us started.

The addict's use has thrown the family into a tizzy for some time. Other members have been hurt and disappointed. They've become angry and resentful. They've learned to react and retaliate. They've wanted to be in control. Instead, they've been pulled into a family disease.

The family solution requires each member to surrender. To let go of resentments. To look for the common good. This is how family recovery begins.

Once again, the alcoholic is named "Father" in this chapter. But it could be the son and brother or the daughter and sister who is the addict. If it helps you in reading this chapter, substitute the term that fits your situation.

Examine the Past

Family members may be surprised that the secret to their recovery lies in looking at the past. My mother used to close the windows when I spoke about treatment. She didn't want the neighbors to hear about our troubles (as if they hadn't already seen them!). But we must make peace with our past. We need to become honest and stop denying our troubles. Doing so also helps us keep in touch with who we are, who we want to become, and who we no longer want to be. As one guy in my group likes to say, "Never get too far away from the puke." That's crass, but wise.

The Big Book also tells us that we can convert our shortcomings into strengths. Our defects motivate our growth through the first nine Steps. They keep us growing in Step Ten. By the Twelfth Step, they've given our lives purpose.

That's the way it is for the addict, and that's the way it is for the family. We owe it to others to share our experience with them. The past becomes a powerful means for the parent or brother or aunt of an addict to reach out to others. They can use it to offer hope and direction. Helping others gives our lives value now. Our past becomes an amazing gift to us and others. *We will not regret the past nor wish to shut the door on it.*

However, beware of your motives in bringing up the past. Make sure you're doing it to help another, not to hurt or humiliate. Draw upon your past for healing.

Alcoholics and addicts are easily hurt. The authors note that we tend to be very sensitive people. That's why love and tolerance are stressed so heavily. We're happier when others treat us with love and tolerance.

Remember the Golden Rule: Do unto others as you would have them do unto you. We know how easily we're hurt, so we can take pains not to hurt others. Rather, we treat them with the same love and tolerance we desire.

Express Yourself

We don't need to suffer silently when hurt by another. We don't need to ignore harmful behavior. But how do we take action without lashing out in anger? Learn to use "I statements."

- Keep the focus on yourself.
- Tell the person how his or her behavior makes you feel.

For example, "When you come home late, I worry."
Or, "When you drive that fast, I'm afraid of being in an accident." Or, "When you yell at me, I feel scared."

This allows us to speak up for ourselves without hurling accusations. We don't put others on the defensive. We can then ask for what we'd like from them, knowing we can't control whether or not they grant our request. We might say, "Please call if you're going to be late." Or, "Please stay within the speed limit." This avoids needless conflict.

The solution works best in a family if each member is willing to look at his or her own issues and work a spiritual program. In giving what we can to the common good of the family, we're likely to receive much more in return.

We addicts need to direct our energies toward repairing

our home life. That's where our addiction usually caused the most damage. Bumper-sticker wisdom applies: "Think globally, act locally." The chance to put this program into action can be found right at home. Sometimes it's easier to be kind to strangers. But our families deserve kindness too. Daily, we can pray for the grace to treat our family with patience, tolerance, and love.

Perfection Not Required

We will not do this perfectly. Don't be discouraged. *We are not saints.* The Big Book reminds us that we all are recovering. Each of us is a work in progress. None of us will ever reach perfection. We need to be patient with one another. Don't focus on the shortcomings. Focus on how far we've come. It took time for our addiction to develop and the family to become sick. It also takes time to heal and recover.

Spirituality First

It can be tempting to throw ourselves into making money. But the Big Book warns that our spiritual life must come first. The rest will follow. It's never the other way around. This is true with money and with other things like studies, fitness, bands, even religion. If we work Step Eleven, the rest will work itself out.

Here's another warning: Watch out for "spiritual intoxication." This is the pink cloud mentioned earlier in the Big Book. It has happened to many of us. We become very caught up in our spiritual experience and try to convert the world. If we keep working the program, this will pass. We start to see that love and tolerance includes respecting others' beliefs.

Something else will likely happen. As our confidence

grows, we won't feel threatened by opposing views. We'll feel secure in our beliefs. We can be comfortable with our concept of God, even if others embrace different concepts.

We need to find balance in our lives. We addicts are compulsive. We tend to be all-or-nothing people. This can tax the patience of our loved ones. The Big Book talks about a father's rush to get back on his feet financially. We may be tempted to rush to catch up in school, jump a fast track on a career, plunge headfirst into a sport or activity, consume a new fad, or devote ourselves to a favorite band. Look for ways to include social, family, and physical activities with your spiritual life. We're not one-dimensional people.

Family members can benefit also from adopting spiritual principles. Al-Anon or Alateen are for family members. Don't expect family members to "get" the program right away. And don't put down family members for how they work their program.

Keep to your side of the street. If each family member does what he or she can to improve the family situation, the family is better off. Be willing to compromise and see things through others' eyes. This will ease conflict and put you back on common ground. Compromise and compassion can pave the way to harmony at home.

Whether you're the addict or the concerned person, getting involved in an organized faith community can support your spiritual growth. Your recovery experience can also be a testament to God's power. Don't let this go to your head. God has worked the miracle, not you. God has done for us what we could not do for ourselves. That honesty humbles us. It lets us put things in their proper place. We get credit for being willing and open to God's grace; God gets credit for working the miracle.

Live a Little

And remember, enjoy life. We've had to do some difficult things—like Steps Four, Five, and Nine. Working the program isn't easy. The Big Book, however, says that laughter is good for us.

Who wouldn't want to enjoy life? Yet, this may not be as easy as it sounds. Fun and play may no longer come naturally. We relied on alcohol and drugs to show us a good time. We may have forgotten how to enjoy ourselves without them. At first, it may require a little work.

I found it helpful to try new activities. I discovered interests I didn't know I had. I took up camping, snowshoeing, kayaking, and photography. You, too, can look for new ways to laugh and have fun: amusement parks, comedy clubs, funny movies. Sports can be a form of play if you don't take the competition too seriously. After a while, you'll find that laughter and fun come naturally. And you'll enjoy life.

The Big Book encourages families to play together. This is a relief after the fear, tension, and resentment we've known. Play can be the family's ticket back to good times. Remember, God wants us to be happy, joyous, and free. Keep this idea close to your heart.

Your Health

Our bodies became dumping grounds for large quantities of alcohol and other drugs. They obviously took their toll. Quitting helped many of us feel better physically, but some health problems may linger. The Big Book recommends getting medical help for those problems.

Sex is another area where qualified professionals can be helpful. Many of us had our first sexual experience while under the influence. Some may never have taken off their clothes with someone else while sober. We relied on alcohol and other drugs to arouse us and calm our inhibitions. We may have done things we're ashamed of. We may have been taken advantage of. If you have concerns about your sexual past, know that you deserve the help and advice of counselors and other safe adults.

Pray for help developing an ideal that reflects your values toward sex. Knowing that we tend toward extremes, be careful not to transfer your energies from drugs to sex. You could end up simply trading obsessions. If you do need help in this area, there are Twelve Step groups that focus on recovery from sexual addictions. Don't hesitate to take advantage of this support. Early recovery can be a time of confusing loneliness. You don't have to go it alone. As stated earlier in this chapter, if you work on your spiritual health, your sexual health is likely to follow.

Words to Live By
Chapter 9 concludes with three slogans for the family's well-being:

- First things first.
- Live and let live.
- Easy does it.

"First things first" means sobriety needs to be the priority. It is most important to cut out the drugs and keep them cut out when dealing with other bad habits.

"Live and let live" means we clean up our side of the street and let others work on their side. We work our program and respect the way others work theirs. We leave their recovery in God's hands just as we entrust our own recovery to our Higher Power. God will do for them what we cannot.

"Easy does it" means we know we're prone to extremes. We try to practice moderation and find balance. We show patience toward ourselves and others.

10

TO EMPLOYERS

Expectations are resentments waiting to happen.

Chapter 10 is written by a businessman. So, what's he got to do with you? It's really not such a stretch if you retitle this chapter "To Teachers" or "To Coaches" or "To Counselors" or "To Adults Everywhere."

This chapter teaches us addicts some things about ourselves. It speaks about our greatest enemies: resentment, jealousy, envy, frustration, and fear. It describes us as energetic people who work and play hard. It stresses the importance of honesty and of working with others. It even calls us smart, imaginative, and likable. It's a chapter worth reading.

And, now, to adults everywhere: If you work with young people, chances are you know an addict or two. Here are some practical suggestions on how to handle addiction from your position of authority. You're in a position to help. The better you understand the disease of addiction, the better you'll be able to help. As someone who cares about kids, you'll benefit from what these pages have to say.

The author begins with a dramatic opening of three suicides. May we avoid being able to say the same ourselves.

Though it's difficult to understand addiction from the sidelines, the Big Book can shed some light on this baffling disease.

For those who aren't recovering themselves, it takes a leap outside of your own experience. There's a giant divide between the moderate drinker and the addict. That was an accurate observation back in the 1930s when the Big Book was written. It remains accurate today. If you're a moderate drinker, the addict probably comes across as careless and foolish. There's nothing in your experience to explain the young addict's repeated harmful behavior.

The divide widens when an adult observes, "It wasn't that way when I was a kid," or "I didn't do that when I was young." If you hear yourself saying this—or even if you simply want to learn more about addiction—I recommend you read chapters 2 and 3 of the Big Book. They describe in more detail how crazy and perplexing this disease is.

That's the first step in understanding addiction: recognizing that it's a disease. The young addict is a sick person. Struggling with the disease, he or she doesn't think or act logically. He or she won't quit using simply to avoid negative consequences.

> The nature of the disease drives addicts to use regardless of what may happen. They place their addiction before all else. It's not a question of bad habits, rebellion, or weakness. They suffer from a disease.

As you read this chapter, consider how the message to employers might apply to you. If you're a teacher or counselor, for instance, there's no direct bottom-line benefit from helping a young addict find the way to recovery. You won't save the cost of training an executive that the author describes, but you will perhaps save a life. That, for most, is enough.

Recently, a high school hockey coach told me about a boy on his team who was a good player but an addict. The boy had suffered another consequence from his use but assured the coach he would stay clean for the season. The coach wondered if he should give him another chance. Sounds a lot like the employer's dilemma, doesn't it?

The coach saw that the team might realize an immediate benefit if the boy played and stayed clean. The coach himself would receive a return on his investment. But the coach also saw the possibility of a greater, long-term benefit for the boy if being on the hockey team gave him incentive to maintain his sobriety. He let the boy play.

In other situations, it might be more appropriate to kick the player off the team. If the addict doesn't seem ready or willing to accept help, or if he or she is determined to keep using, the coach might be doing the player a favor by kicking him or her off the team. The consequence sends a message about the behavior. Moreover, it can provide motivation to change. It could help the addict reach bottom and become ready to change.

The young addict you know has probably gone to great lengths to conceal his or her use. An addict can be a master of deceit. Dishonesty is one symptom of this disease. He or she may also try to take advantage of you. Manipulation goes hand in hand with addiction. Although these behaviors are symptoms of the disease, they call for consequences.

But if the addict does want to quit, you can help. You might say how you have heard about the person's use. Be as specific as possible about what you've heard and the consequences associated with his or her use. Maybe you've heard only rumors, nothing you can prove. Admit this, but add that usually such rumors have some basis in fact, which is why you're concerned. State that you believe he or she is in trouble with alcohol or drugs. If it applies, tell the person that you appreciate his or her abilities. Add that you value or care about him or her if this is true but that you cannot keep him or her on the team, in the dorm—whatever fits—if the use continues.

Explain that addiction is a disease, just as the Big Book describes.

It's wise to advise the young addict from the get-go that recovery—rather than just quitting for a short period of time—will require a new attitude and way of thinking.

Pay close attention to your "baloney detector" when you listen to the addict's response. If he or she triggers it, and you think the person is trying to snow you, trust that. Lay down the law and spell out the consequences of another confirmed use. Be prepared to follow through.

But if you sense that the addict is sincere and you're satisfied by his or her willingness, help him or her to develop a plan. Treatment might be a good option. Treatment can jumpstart recovery. It's no replacement for AA and the solution outlined in previous chapters, but it can be a good beginning. Treatment provides the addict with the tools of recovery; AA teaches the addict how to use them. If treatment isn't an option, steer the person directly to AA.

You may already know a treatment center that works with young adults. If not, consult your school counselor or the yellow pages under "Alcoholism." To find AA, see the white pages under "Alcoholics Anonymous." If there's no listing, refer to appendix 6 on page 573 of the Big Book for other suggestions on finding a group in your area.

The addict may ask you not to tell others. You can probably promise this within reason. For instance, if you're a guidance counselor, you may not have to tell the student's teachers and coaches about the situation. Let the student do so when he or she is ready and willing. You will, however, need to discuss the situation with the student's parents. Be careful not to let on otherwise. The parents must be involved in the solution, unless their own use is so severe that it poses a threat to the student.

You can set up a meeting with the addict, his or her parents, and you, where the addict can lay out the problem and ask for help. You can suggest the next steps to take in getting help. You can also educate the parents about addiction. Reassure them that their child's condition is not because of any failing on their or their child's part. It's a disease. You can also attest to the solution described in the Big Book. Offer them a copy to read. Let them know help is available. Provide what you can when they ask for it.

They might not ask. This approach will work for some, not for others. You cannot control the outcome. All you can do is lead the horse to water. But, to do so, you must know where to find the water.

When the young addict returns from treatment, you can provide additional support. You can offer an ear. To solicit trust, promise confidentiality unless the person talks about hurting himself or herself or others. Before you have a discussion, inform him or her that you're required by law in most states to report any threats of self-harm or harm to others. This caveat will prevent an awkward and trust-shattering situation after the addict has opened up. It also can be a way for the addict to ask for further help when he or she knows no other way.

Whenever possible, put the young addict in touch with other recovering addicts in your community. Many schools have support groups for such students. Recommend AA as well.

The chapter talks about office politics. Replace that term with social cliques, and you've got pretty much the same dynamic. The young addict is bound to struggle with resentment, jealousy, envy, frustration, and fear. Paranoia may also be an issue. You can offer an objective perspective and provide reality checks. You can also help by educating others within the community about the nature of the disease and the importance of love and tolerance in a young person's recovery.

Encourage balance and moderation in the young person's life but hold a light rein. Let him or her make a fresh start. Given the right amount of support and having the willingness to work a spiritual program, many young addicts will recover. Once they have a firm foundation, you can enlist their help in working with other young addicts. This will greatly benefit their recovery.

The authors suggest that you trust addicts until they give you reason not to. But what to do if they slip? If it's truly a slip—short-term use and not a full-blown relapse—addicts may benefit from a second chance. The most natural thing in the world is for an addict to use. That's not to say you spare the consequences laid out earlier. But if addicts are open afterward about their slip, their honesty can be a gauge to their commitment to recovery and whether you should continue trying to help. If they're still hedging on the truth, they probably aren't ready. You may need to let go of them.

If you work in a school, you might think of the teachers as the junior executives, the ones in direct contact with the potential addicts. You can suggest they read the Big Book to better understand addiction and those with whom they're working. If they do read it, they may be more open-minded about helping the addict. So, too, might you.

11

A VISION FOR YOU

Loneliness is curable.

This chapter tells the story of AA's beginnings. The book was written less than five years after AA began in 1935. Alcoholics Anonymous had only a few groups. Membership was small. The Big Book was the primary means of spreading the word about the program.

The founders of AA outlined the program in these first eleven chapters. Their goal was to tell newcomers everything they needed to know about getting sober. The plan of action is all there. These days, AA meetings abound. They're held every day in cities around the world, but the original plan of action still works as well today as it did then.

For many of us, those last days of using were awful. We were haunted by what the Big Book calls the Four Horsemen: Terror, Bewilderment, Frustration, Despair. We were lonely and ready for the friendship and understanding found at meetings.

The authors promise that the Fellowship will free you from your cares, boredom, and worry. You'll find out what it means to love your neighbor as yourself.

Not So Different

"I don't know," you might say. "I'm different. I'm *fill in the blank*. Maybe you're younger, black, addicted to crank, smarter, growing up in a different age. Whatever. Perhaps you suffer from a case of "terminal uniqueness," the sense that you're just not like others. Me too. I was always looking for the way I was different from others. In AA, I met a bunch of people like me. We all suffered from a sense of terminal uniqueness, which kept others at arm's length. Once we realized that we were more alike than different, we could help and understand one other.

Now, obviously, there's no one else *exactly* like you. But when we focus on what we have in common, we can reap the benefits of the Fellowship. If we continue to believe that we're too different—for whatever reason—we sentence ourselves to the misery of isolation. That's where the terminal part comes in. Without others, we're dead. We thought we were different when we were using, but we can't hold on to this belief in recovery. The solution, as we know it, requires us to share our experience of addiction and recovery.

We find that we have plenty in common with other addicts, right down to our thinking that we're all different. Our common experience lets us support one another's recovery.

In this chapter, we run into Bill W., whose story you read in the first chapter. He was in Akron, Ohio, when his addict mind tried to ambush him. It's a great setup, him in the hotel lobby with the bar at one end and the church directory at the other. The devil on one shoulder is whispering, "Wouldn't it feel good to have just three drinks, no more?" The angel on the other shoulder says, "You know where you'll end up if you do. Once you start, you can't stop."

He's got to choose: addiction or recovery? He chooses recovery, but he realizes what he must do to stay sober. He must find another alcoholic to help. He must find someone else like him to whom he can reach out. That's his lifeline to recovery.

Bill met Dr. Bob, and he didn't drink that day. Seeking out another alcoholic to help worked. That became the foundation of the AA program.

Later Bill and Bob sought out a third alcoholic to help. This third alcoholic was Bill D. These three men made up the first AA group. AA was born June 1935 in Akron, Ohio. (You can learn more of the early origins of AA by reading the stories of Dr. Bob and Bill D. in the second section of the Big Book.)

When Bill W. and Dr. Bob laugh at Bill D.'s description of his hopeless condition, they don't mean to make fun of him. Rather, they laugh in recognition. Bill D. thinks he's different. He thinks he's hopeless in a way Bill W. and Dr. Bob can't understand. They laugh. They had felt that way themselves. They're happy to tell him what they have in common and that, yes, there's hope for him too.

It works. Bill D. has a spiritual experience and recovers from his addiction.

You might think that this AA program is only for white businessmen like the first three members. But then we meet the fourth member of AA. He was a reckless and careless young guy, perhaps more like yourself. And, eventually, women joined the Fellowship as well.

Those early AA meetings were held in members' living rooms or around kitchen tables. They all, regardless of their backgrounds, found a safe place where fellow addicts understood them like few others could. They found a place where they could laugh at their troubles and learn to overcome them.

> Hope is a four-letter word.

A Worldwide Bond

The founders were proud of AA's early growth. Back then a small community may have had fifteen members. Now AA has two million members worldwide. The miracles God has worked through AA have far exceeded the founders' expectations.

When the authors wrote the Big Book, they wanted to spread the word. And they did. The Big Book has been translated into forty-three languages. Today, AA meetings are held in more than 150 countries. There are more than 100,000 AA groups worldwide.

The Big Book is intended to be a starting place. The advice is offered as mere suggestions. Readers are told to turn to God, who offers constant guidance. Read this book, keep asking what God wants for you, and you're off to a wonderful beginning.

On page 164, the program is summarized in the second to the last paragraph. We're told to do these things:

- Surrender to God.
- Admit your shortcomings.
- Clean up your past messes.
- Help others.

The Big Book's authors have all since passed away, but they remain with us in spirit. They paved us a way for a happy destiny. Pass it on, and you'll stay on that road with them.

12

MY CHANCE TO LIVE

*People don't come into AA because
they're having a happy life.*

On page 309 of the Big Book, we meet a girl who could've been me. Like her, I grew up in a good home. I had an alcoholic grandfather but thought I could avoid the addiction gene. I ended up taking the express train to dependency. We both walked into AA at seventeen. She and I have many similarities.

She calls herself a "walking contradiction," tough on the outside, tender on the inside. Ready to lash out before she could get hurt. That was her best defense. She felt so vulnerable that she wanted to protect herself. I carefully burrowed under my own defenses, trying to shield my vulnerabilities. I showed one face to the world and kept the other to myself. That's common with us addicts.

She wanted to survive adolescence, which tormented her. Once an adult, she figured things would get easier. In the meantime, her teenage years seemed unbearable. She tried to black them out. When she drank, she had blackouts—periods of time she couldn't remember. Those blackouts were one sign of addiction. But they didn't bother her.

She ached to fit in but feared she never would. Instead, she found a friend in alcohol. It worked. Drinking gave her friends and brought her fun. It even turned getting into trouble into a good thing. Not many adults will admit this when giving their "drinking is dangerous" lecture to teenagers. Yet teenagers aren't stupid. They drink, have fun, and think, "Yeah, baby." That's how it was for me, how it was for her. Alcohol worked.

Alcohol Took Away Her Sky

But it didn't work forever. She did things that went against her value system and that ate at her self-esteem. It hurt her to make her mom cry. She almost got thrown out of school. Her answer to these problems was to drink more, but that only made things worse. Within two years, alcohol had betrayed her—it had taught her to fly but then took away the sky. Addiction can happen that quickly in adolescence.

She says she didn't realize that she had lost the choice to stop drinking. I was just like that. I'd heard so many pro athletes and other celebrities talk about beating their drug habits that I figured I could quit too, if I had to. It didn't occur to me that it might not be so easy.

There's something else. As a teenager, I thought I was immortal—that nothing could hurt me. I thought major problems, including addiction, would bounce off me. The author runs through her list of reasons why she couldn't be an addict, her variations on saying, "Not me." I'd started that with my first drunk, when I walked a straight line along the carpet to prove I wouldn't have the problems others had when drunk. But, by seventeen, I could no longer cling to my defense that I was too young. Like this girl, I wasn't old enough to drink legally, but I was old enough to be an alcoholic and addict.

When she started out, drinking was fun. That good time gave way to bad times. Then, when she was working as a waitress, she met the recovering alcoholics who were having a good time. That appealed to her. On her night off, she missed their laughter. That was the beginning of her recovery: She recognized something she wanted in those who were sober.

She says she never intended to end up in AA. Who does?

Instead of committing to a lifetime of sobriety, she tried to find a quick fix. She figured if she quit drinking for a little while, she could straighten things out enough so she could drink again. When I wound up in detox, I figured I could quit for three months and be ready to drink again by New Year's Eve. I didn't want to give up that special drunk my senior year of high school. But, like the author, after about three months, I realized how stupid this was.

She says she "hit bottom." In other words, things got so bad, she didn't want them to get worse. That was when she was ready to surrender. We all have to get to this point before we're willing to try a way other than our own.

> Hope is what's left over after you lose everything.

In her case—as in mine—it was a "high bottom." We didn't bounce in and out of institutions. We didn't lose careers, marriages, and children. We didn't do irreparable damage to our livers. We didn't risk wet brain. We were too young for that; our using career was too short. We skipped the advanced stages of addiction, but we were miserable enough to know we didn't want to prolong our misery.

She was angry that the bottom hit her so young. She felt cheated. Me too. I had looked forward to glory days of college drinking. I wanted to be able to party without a curfew. I wanted to live in a dorm where I could keep my bong and a bottle on my desk. But I had to let go of those fantasies.

The Gift of Choice

It helped to discover that I could have fun sober. That's also what sold the author on AA. A summer spent hanging out with sober people who enjoyed life convinced her that they had what she wanted. She had lost the fun of drinking but discovered that the elusive joy she desired could be found through recovery.

I like her image of AA as a ladder with twelve steps that could lead her out of the dark hole she had sunk into. In order to get out, she had to work the Steps. There was no easier, softer way—even though she looked for it. And no one else could climb that ladder for her. She had to work the program herself. She had to be willing, and she had to take action. She was, and she did.

Once she did, she was rewarded with an inner peace. That's quite a contrast to the confusion and despair she described earlier. AA also gave her the gift of choice. Addiction had taken that away. The Twelve Steps restored it.

But, of course, her cure didn't happen overnight. She admits that in the beginning, her emotions overwhelmed her. She suffered through emotional highs and lows along with plenty of confusion. That's the way it is in early recovery.

I remember seeing a feelings chart in treatment. The poster pictured different faces labeled with feelings like "happy," "sad," or "jealous." It's taken me years to be able to match my own feelings with their faces. It's taken me years to let my outsides reflect my insides.

So, too, the author. But she's finally there. She describes another reward of being willing and taking action to work the Steps. Once a person so depressed she tried to kill herself, she eventually found herself at peace with herself and the world.

I can think of no better endorsement for AA.

13

STUDENT OF LIFE

*In order to stay sober, I've got to be
willing to be part of my own life.*

The authors of the Big Book call alcohol "cunning, baffling, powerful." On page 319 of the Big Book, we meet a woman who calls alcohol a lie. It's a seductive lie, one we want to believe. Once we do, we hang on to that lie even though it could kill us. That's why getting honest is so critical to our recovery. This woman finally discovered the truth—and saw alcohol for the lie it was—when she attended AA. And the truth set her free.

She admits that she started drinking late—at eighteen—but that once she did, she had an *aha!* moment that changed her life. By the time she graduated from high school, she was terrified, insecure, and unable to understand her emotions. That description fits many high school kids, but the insecurity and terror seem intensified in the addict. Many of us are extremely sensitive, perceptive, and feel things deeply. She confesses, "I always felt as if everyone else knew what was going on and what they were supposed to be doing. . . ."

That's a fitting description of adolescence. To me, everyone else seemed at ease, yet my guts churned. I couldn't imagine that they felt tortured by the same insecurity and confusion.

Then, her first night at college, she found the answer to her problems. She drank, got drunk—and it was wonderful! She could dance, talk, and enjoy being in her own skin. Even when hungover the next morning and clutching the porcelain prayer stool, she thought, *This is it!*

Later, she realizes that the addict mind had already taken hold of her with that first drunk. Her addict mind was whispering that sweet lie, *I can make you feel better. Trust me.*

She wanted to believe it was true even when circumstances argued otherwise. When her grades slipped, she blamed the difficulty of her courses and switched majors. When others expressed concern over her using, she rationalized that she was simply partying like college kids did.

You can rationalize just about anything, as she did, but those rationalizations keep the lie alive. They become the cornerstone in the fortress of our denial. They block us from the truth.

This woman didn't come from an alcoholic family, so she hadn't witnessed the horrors of drinking up close. Nor did her DNA conspire against her by passing along the inheritance of addiction. That's worth noting. It's true that children of alcoholics or addicts are at greater risk of becoming addicted. But you don't have to come from a family of addicts to become one yourself. There are addiction pioneers in every family. This woman was one in hers.

Nursing a Lie

After graduating from college, she planned to "drink properly" but was surprised when she couldn't. Ask any college student who's been binge drinking (consuming five or more drinks at one time). They'll tell you, "I'll quit when I want." Some can. Alcoholics can't. The difference is, alcoholics don't know they can't. They suffer the delusion that they can and will settle down at any time. Yet it's not so easy.

This young woman developed a familiar routine, drinking every evening by herself in front of the television until she passed out. She supported her habit by stealing from her parents and protected her supply by stashing bottles. She worked hard to deceive her parents—and herself—about the amount she drank by not throwing bottles in the trash. She nursed the lie.

After a couple years of misery, she tried graduate school, attempting a geographic cure. She believed a change of scenery would bring about a change in her use. It's common for addicts to seek these "geographics." They overlook that they bring themselves along—wherever they go, there their problems are.

That was her story. She slowed her drinking for a few months but eventually returned to her routine of getting smashed in front of the television. She had thought she might have a problem and watched the movie of Bill W.'s life out of curiosity, whiskey in hand. She managed to convince herself she wasn't an alcoholic by comparing herself to Bill and saying, "I'm not that bad."

That worked for me too. I looked around at friends who used more often, who used harder drugs, or who had gotten into more trouble. I said, "See, I'm not that bad." You can always find someone worse off than yourself to justify your use. That's just another rationalization. Another rationalization that buttresses the fortress of denial.

She took an alcoholism quiz to better convince herself. Ever lose a job due to your drinking? Nope. Spouse? Nope.

Children? Nope. She was relieved to be able to answer no so often. Of course, she hadn't had jobs, spouses, or children to lose, but that was beside the point. She could tell herself she wasn't an alcoholic, even though she knew she said so with her fingers crossed behind her back.

Lonely and Defeated

Of course, her drinking got worse. She started earlier and drank more. She was a quiet, daily drinker. Her first drunk had let her dance and enjoy herself, but drinking now isolated her from the world. She could still say that she hadn't had any of the traditional problems associated with alcoholism. She hadn't been arrested, hadn't picked fights, hadn't cracked up her car. She may not have caused any problems in society, but she had stirred up plenty of internal trouble. Alcohol had left her lonely and defeated.

Yet, perhaps because she hadn't had these traditional consequences, she didn't think her drinking was to blame. She thought she was insane.

She glimpsed the truth the afternoon she sat on the couch and *knew* she was going to drink again in spite of herself. She knew without wanting to admit what was wrong.

Finally, she met another alcoholic, the Hawaiian sales rep, who took her to AA. She had known about AA but avoided it because she didn't think she was as bad off as *those people.* Her rationalizations kept her away.

The turning point for her came when she told her story at her second AA meeting. She peered over the podium and saw the face of AA listening to her. She saw the face of understanding, empathy, and love. She saw the face of God.

That was a significant spiritual experience for her. *This,* she discovered, is the answer. Not alcohol. *This*—what she found in AA—was what she'd been looking for. The thought came to her in a moment of sober clarity to be trusted more than what she had believed in her hangover fuzz. The truth exposed the earlier lie that alcohol was the answer. And it brought her relief.

This woman did three important things for her sobriety right off. She went to meetings, found a sponsor, and joined a home group. That secured her sobriety.

Ninety in Ninety

She attended ninety meetings in ninety days, one meeting a day for three months. It's a common prescription for newcomers. Rather than go wherever it was they went to use daily, they go to AA. The meetings become their new routine. They provide a means of absorbing the program, of surrounding themselves with support in the early shaky days, and of establishing a foundation of sobriety.

A sponsor is someone who has more time in the program and can share what he or she has learned about working the Steps. Having a sponsor is like having a personal tutor in the program, something this "student of life" took to readily. The sponsor can show the newcomer how to live the program.

In finding a sponsor, look for someone who seems to be enjoying sobriety and who has that special something you want out of life. AA recommends that men seek out male sponsors and women seek out female sponsors to avoid romantic complications. (To learn more about sponsorship, read the AA pamphlet *Questions and Answers on Sponsorship.*)

She also found a "home group." A home group is one that you attend regularly and perhaps the group where you become most involved. It usually becomes the group where you experience the fellowship of AA most intimately. You commit to this group, and it becomes your anchor in AA, regardless of how many other meetings you might attend. A home group becomes that special place where everybody knows your name and where you truly do feel at home—without having to drink to get there.

> Here's the good news about recovery: You've got to feel your feelings. Here's the bad news about recovery: You've got to feel your feelings.

The author says she rode a roller coaster of early recovery. That's a common description. We don't just quit using and suddenly live happily ever after. On the contrary, life usually becomes pretty damn hard. We're hit by a swirl of emotions that we're no longer numbing with drugs. There's a sudden change in lifestyle. We've left behind our using buddies and are meeting new people. They might be friendly but still they're strangers. We're trying to work this program we're still struggling to understand. We don't yet know how to handle situations that had been occasions to get high. Early recovery is a baffling and bewildering time. Every day seems like the first day at a new school.

So, attending lots of meetings, finding a sponsor, and establishing a home group provide comfort on the confusing roller-coaster ride.

The author says that in working the Steps she has gained friends and learned how to be a friend. She's learned about intimacy with her boyfriend of five years. And she's gained a friend in herself. She no longer believes alcohol is the answer. She's discovered the way of AA.

14

TIGHTROPE

We're as sick as our secrets.

On page 359 we meet a man with a secret. A secret kept this man sick longer than he needed to be. It complicated his disease and closed him off from others. Once he was willing to be open and honest in AA, he realized he didn't have to be afraid of his sexuality and he no longer had to be alone.

He refers to himself at the time he went off to college as "an alcoholic waiting to happen." He was smart but shy and lonely, vulnerable emotionally and socially. No wonder he fell in love with alcohol. Drinking transformed him. He could hide his fears and speak easily with others. The way alcohol transforms our personalities is another trait common to alcoholics. At first that transformation can be very agreeable. We like what drinking does for us.

This man didn't like the taste of alcohol, but he loved the effects. That's telling. He wasn't drinking for the enjoyment but for the result. He was willing to put up with what he didn't like so he could get the payoff. That's often another signpost pointing toward addiction.

He drank to deny his sexuality. He drank to deny the truth

about himself. He pretended to be straight. He lived a lie. When he did express himself sexually with other men, he felt unnecessary guilt and shame. So he drank more.

Out of Control

He was open with some gay friends but continued pretending with those straight people whom he feared wouldn't accept him. That put him on the tightrope he mentions. He lived in terror of falling off. When he became involved in a serious relationship, he quit his law practice rather than be honest.

He made a promise to himself that he couldn't keep. After having a blackout, he promised he'd quit if he had another. He had another blackout. And another. And another. But he kept drinking. He couldn't quit. His drinking was out of control.

So was he. His personality changed more radically when he drank, and not in pleasant ways. He said nasty things when drunk or swung to the other extreme, becoming overly charming and affectionate. He became unpredictable when drunk.

When he was growing up, his family had certain rules for drinking. So long as you could hold down a job, not embarrass the family, and stay out of trouble, you could get drunk regularly. The rules about drinking were about managing the consequences. But he couldn't do that, either.

Drinking cost him his relationship and other friendships. It made him increasingly paranoid and resentful, not necessarily qualities one looks for in a friend or lover. His loneliness deepened. He got beaten and robbed. He stole tips to pay for drinks. He got kicked out of bars.

Having failed the family rules, he started to drink alone at home. This guy, bright enough to do well in law school, was reduced to someone afraid to ride buses or even walk down the street. He became a fall-down drunk who feared leaving home. He lived in a pigsty littered with empty food containers and overrun by mice. He became someone people avoided. Fear and self-pity ruled him.

He realized how out of control he was when he couldn't stick to his plan to have one drink after work, then go directly home. After that one drink, he blacked out and wound up in a stranger's bed. The next morning, he saw in the stranger's look of disgust and pity how far down he had slid. He saw what he'd become, and he didn't like what he saw. He realized that once he started drinking, he couldn't control how much he drank or what happened to him.

Burdens Begin to Lift

But his thinking was so messed up that he still believed drinking was holding his life together. The people he met in AA told him he didn't have to drink again. At first, he couldn't imagine life without alcohol, though he certainly didn't want to keep living the life he was in.

They also told him he didn't have to be alone anymore. Again, he didn't really believe them at first, but he wanted to. He had had enough of his miserable, alcohol-imposed isolation.

This man had fallen in love with alcohol from the start; it took AA longer to win him over. He objected, argued, questioned, and doubted many aspects of the program. His sponsor was wise to be patient with him.

The author of this chapter stalled at the idea of God. It was a revelation to him that he could doubt God, especially coming from the mouth of his sponsor, a minister in real life. That cracked his agnosticism, which, in his case, was simply another form of denial. He did believe in a Higher Power; he just wouldn't let himself at first.

He started with the idea that there might be a God but it wasn't him. He let go of that selfish desire to run the show. He also decided to "act as if." He acted as if he did believe in God. This most likely meant he prayed and turned over his will, even if he wasn't convinced there was a God on the other end. With time, he found the program's ideals as coming from God. He could accept as a Higher Power the love that flowed through AA meetings and members' lives.

Reach Out

Early on, he complained to his sponsor that other members weren't more outgoing. His sponsor wisely suggested he become more outgoing himself, perhaps by making the coffee at his meeting. He did it, at first to select better cookies for himself, but eventually the strategy worked. The service position put him in touch with other group members.

That's a simple trick you might try yourself. It could be making coffee, but it doesn't have to be. It could be emptying ashtrays, setting up chairs, cleaning up after meetings, being a greeter, reading "How It Works," offering rides, serving as a temporary sponsor, and so on. There are many ways to become more involved and reap the benefits of the Fellowship.

When he was not yet three years into sobriety, this man's life took a turn for the worse. His health failed, his father died, and AIDS wiped out half of his gay friends. That's the way it goes sometimes. Shit happens. Things can get worse in sobriety. It's false to believe otherwise. Life doesn't stop. It goes on and brings its share of hardship and struggle— sometimes all at once. We can't control that. But we can reach out for help. That's what this man did. He turned to his Higher Power. He asked for help and received it.

This could be you too. When life gets tough, you may want

to escape the pain by getting drunk or high. On the other hand, the spiritual support of the Fellowship and your Higher Power can see you through in ways drinking and drugging can't. We need not suffer alone.

> Remember, there's no problem that using can't make worse.

No More Pretending

This man felt accepted in AA as a gay man. He didn't need to hide his identity. He could stop pretending. AA loved him as he was and let him down from the tightrope gently. That's the Fellowship working.

He doesn't speak at length about how he came to terms with himself and his sexuality in sobriety. If you're in a similar situation, questioning or confused about your orientation, seek out a gay member in your group with more sobriety. Choose someone you trust and with whom you can speak candidly. If it helps you to feel more comfortable, invite your sponsor along. Have an open discussion about your sexuality in a setting that's not sexually charged. It can help to talk with more than one person. It's also helpful to talk to counselors or other trusted adults about your sexuality questions. Don't isolate yourself.

We're on a journey of self-discovery and acceptance—our sexuality is but one area for us to explore and affirm. Others are willing to help.

Although it took this man awhile to warm up to AA, he admits that after twelve years he has developed a deep and intimate relationship with the program. He's no longer alone. He has found an extended family in the Fellowship.

15

WINDOW OF OPPORTUNITY

Easy does it, but do it.

On page 421 we meet a man who thought he had to be somebody else to be loved and accepted. So he pretended. But alcohol and drugs shoved him further away from what he wanted. In the emergency room after he walked through a window, he pushed away those trying to care for him with his self-centered, arrogant behavior. The nurse described him as the most obnoxious person she'd ever met. It wasn't until he met love and acceptance in AA that he could be himself.

Like many alcoholics and addicts, he felt different. Ironically, that's how we're alike—we all feel different. But he didn't know then what he had in common with other addicts. He believed because he was different, others wouldn't like him. So he schemed for their love, affirmation, and attention with his charm and quick jokes.

When he was a kid, his parents bullied him to be good. If he could just hang on until he turned eighteen, he figured, he'd be free. He figured a change in his situation would make things better. He was betting on a geographic cure.

But when he got to college, he again felt different. He felt ashamed of his background and who he was. Worse, he feared that others wouldn't like him if they knew who he really was.

Double Lives

Many of us know that fear only too well. We feel like a cheat, perhaps because we live double lives while using. For whatever reason, we're terrified that others will discover us as a fraud. We are ashamed of who we are and live in fear that they'll reject us once they discover the truth about us.

He was a smart, funny, likable guy afraid of others abandoning him if they knew who he truly was. It's sad that so many of us believe this and live in the same fear. We go to such lengths to hide who we are. He would have to hit bottom before he came to believe he was okay as is.

In this guy's case, many of his insecurities revolved around money. He wasn't unique. Most of us have money issues. Money is a lot like sex. It can be tricky and confusing. It can dominate our lives and destroy relationships. In recovery, we need to come to terms with these issues—or they could lead us to use again.

Some of us blame money. After all, "Money is the root of all evil." But, in fact, the Bible passage reads, "The love of money is the root of all evil" (I Timothy 6:10, King James version). The problem lies with our attitude. Our narrator equated money with security, prestige, and worth. What does money represent for you? What role does it play in your life? Are you comfortable with its place in your life?

Doing a Fifth Step on money could help you sort out these

issues. Ask yourself, where have you been selfish, dishonest, or inconsiderate in relation to money? Whom did you hurt? This inventory could help you in shaping a sane and sound ideal of money. We pray for guidance in shaping this ideal and for the strength to live by it. As with any issue, we turn it over to our Higher Power.

Back to our hero at college. He not only pretended to be wealthy, he also pretended to be an accomplished, veteran drinker. Again, he was afraid that if others found out the truth about him—that he had never been drunk—they'd abandon him. Dependent upon others' approval, he was desperate to impress others.

His was a quick descent into addiction. Within three months, he was drinking daily. Three more months, and he was drugging daily. Alcohol and drugs wiped out his dreams and goals. Yet he was willing to give up almost everything to keep drinking and drugging. Alcohol and drugs took priority in his life, which, predictably, became unmanageable.

Lowered Goals

He makes a wise observation about alcoholics. He says the nonalcoholic will do whatever it takes to get what he or she wants. The alcoholic or addict, on the other hand, will claim to want less to keep using. Although he was once an "A" student, his drinking caused him to skip class, neglect homework, and almost flunk out of school. He simply lowered his goals to allow himself to continue using.

Things finally got so bad that he worked out a desperate deal with the dean. But once he had dodged the bullet, he broke his promise. Once the hangover—physical or emotional—has passed, we're willing to risk it again. Or, once the threat is gone, we're willing to again place ourselves in harm's way. That's a trick of our addict mind, another symptom of our insanity.

> We addicts suffer a peculiar sort of amnesia. Once we're out of immediate danger, we tend to forget how bad things were.

This guy told the dean, "I'll be okay on my own." Those are famous last words for an addict. Two weeks later, he plunged through that second-story window and into a five-day coma. His use brought him this close to death.

When he hit that concrete window well, he bottomed out—literally and figuratively. But he wasn't willing to lose school. He put that before his use. So he cut another deal with the dean: He would go to AA if doing so would give him a second chance at school.

For me, losing my parents' approval and respect became more important than using. Their disappointment crushed me. I remember the expression on their faces one morning after I had stayed out all night getting high and drunk. I stumbled into our house at about six A.M. and saw my parents sitting there worried sick. They'd been up for hours, fretting over me. The fear and anger showed on their faces.

I finally remembered that look the last night I got wasted. I had wound up in detox and figured I would bust out, hitchhike home, and sneak into our house. Because of this plan I wouldn't tell the authorities my name. One of them cracked my delusion with the question, "Don't you think your parents might be wondering where you are?"

I looked at the clock. It read quarter to six, and that look on my parents' faces came back to me. I didn't want to do that to them again. I told the authorities my name, and it turned out my parents had been up again, worried about me. The desire not to cause them further pain outweighed my desire to use again. That helped me stay sober those early days.

The narrator felt he had bottomed out in AA. To his family's way of thinking, winding up in AA was a disgrace similar to being sent to prison. He had messed up in a way that cost him his honor and dignity. Or so he thought. In AA, he expected to meet bums who had crawled out of the gutter propped up in folding chairs. Instead, he found a respectable and happy group of people talking about God. Surprise.

An Apple Trying to Be an Orange

His first *aha!* in AA was that he had been an apple trying to be an orange. That's how he came to understand his pattern of pretending and his fear of rejection. He realized he was an apple among apples. That was okay. He no longer had to pretend.

He admits that his stubbornness slowed his progress at first. Others made suggestions for his recovery that he refused to follow. He refused to travel to meetings outside his neighborhood, which meant he could attend only two meetings a week. He refused to stay out of relationships in the early months. He refused to find a sponsor. He refused to seek a Higher Power. He thought he was smarter than the others and that he could do it better than they could.

That junkie thinking keeps us stuck. It almost killed this guy. His emotions swung from paralyzing despair to murderous rage. He wanted to kill himself.

His turning point came when he was willing to be open and honest with another person. When he shared his feelings with another man in the one-on-one meeting he describes, he defeated his fear of being abandoned. Quite courageously, he bared his insides. The other alcoholic, rather than leave our guy worthless and alone, met him with acceptance and love. That's the Fellowship. The narrator realized he was good enough as he was and that he no longer had to fear being found out as a fraud.

He also made a significant discovery when the other man told him he didn't have to drink over situations. He had found love and acceptance, but that discovery gave him hope. No matter what happened, he didn't have to drink.

With hope in hand, he changed. He prayed. He worked the Steps. He found a sponsor. He became active in his home group. In short, he started doing what others suggested, and—what do you know?—it worked. His sobriety started. Up to that point, he had been dry. Once he started working the program, he began his recovery.

Many Paths to the Top of the Mountain

But, of course, it wasn't "happily ever after." When he headed to law school, he didn't like the way people there approached AA. He complained that they weren't doing it right. Rather, they weren't doing it his way. His sponsor asked, "Are they sober?" This reminds us that there isn't just one way to work the program. There are many paths to the top of the mountain.

Each AA group has its own personality, influenced by its setting and culture. We can become accustomed to a certain flavor of AA, especially the one we encountered when we first got sober. It can be unsettling to find the flavor has changed when we expected it to be the same, sort of like sitting in your car after someone else has driven it. Things just don't feel right. But that's what gives AA its richness. If the people in that meeting are staying sober, it's working for them—and could work for you too. Chances are, their way will enrich your program.

The narrator eventually found his way with his new group. He learned to unplug his ears and listen to the other members. Rather than try to impose his way, he was willing to learn theirs. And he found God at work—in them, and in him.

> Hearing is often the first thing to go in an addict. We can't hear others' concern for us, and we can't hear the truth.

His life has become one of joy. That nineteen-year-old punk who crashed through a second-story window has become a grateful recovering alcoholic, a devoted husband, and a loving father. By the grace of God, he lives a full and rich life. He no longer fears being worthless and alone. Recovery has brought him the love and acceptance he desired.

16

A VISION OF RECOVERY

*I'm not where I want to be, but thank
God I'm not where I was.*

We meet a red-headed Native American on page 494 of the
Big Book. Usually, the feeling of being inferior goes hand in
hand with the feeling of being different. This guy played the
part of the tough guy, directed by alcohol and drugs. In the
end, he learned compassion, how to get outside of himself
and sympathize with others. But it was a long, painful road.

He says he loved the feeling of complete freedom that alcohol gave him. It released him from his cares and worries,
let him do what he wanted. He liked that. Who wouldn't? Yet
he saw the danger in drinking. As a young boy, he was scared
by his father's drunken rages. He swore he'd be different. He
didn't swear off drinking. He just swore he wouldn't be a
nasty drunk. Of course, it isn't that easy. Alcoholics who
drink can't control their behavior. This guy not only ends up
like his father as an alcoholic, he also becomes frightening
with his drunken rages. It's a tale told by many alcoholics.
They see the damage caused by a parent's drinking and vow
they won't let that happen to them. But it does. They can't

control the addiction. How important did alcohol become to him? His dying mother needs him to give her medicine, but he's preoccupied by thoughts of getting drunk with his friends. He loves his mother, but his need for alcohol has become stronger than his feelings for even her. That's how powerful alcohol is.

Beer-Colored Lenses

Alcohol can misplace our affections. It can distort our perspective. Looking at life through beer-colored lenses, we become shortsighted. All we see before us is the next chance to get drunk. We lose sight of the bigger picture and what we truly care about.

After his mom dies, he feels shame and remorse. He really did love her. He drinks to wash away those feelings. For a short time, the alcohol helps him forget. But drinking isn't a permanent solution. It won't bring back his mother. It can't undo what he's done. It can't erase the shame and remorse. And it can't forgive him.

He repeats this behavior with his son. Again, he loves his son. He's proud of him. Deep down, he wants to care about his son more than he cares about alcohol. But his relationship with alcohol has become the primary relationship in his life. He's more faithful to alcohol than to his son. He winds up drunk instead of taking his son to the movies, as promised.

Think back on your using days. Are they littered with broken promises? Are they littered with times when you put your relationship with drugs or alcohol before your personal relationships? When you cared more about getting high than the feelings of those you loved? Addiction will do that to you. It takes away our ability to keep our word.

The more this guy drinks, the more he feels guilt, remorse,

and fear. But, as much as he dislikes those feelings, he isn't ready to stop drinking. Now, he shakes his head at his craziness. Alcohol had so distorted his thinking that he drinks in the hospital after having his lung punctured during a drunken fight. He can see with the clarity of sobriety how blurry his vision had become.

He tries various ways to stop the consequences of his drinking. Nothing works until he tries AA. Why does AA work for him when nothing else does? For starters, he finds hope in the Twelve Steps. He believes they can help make his life better. He also is willing to believe in a Higher Power.

Even though he's not sure at first what to make of the Higher Power, he gets by on his faith in the program and his willingness to believe. He searches sincerely to gain an understanding of his Higher Power. He looks into his own tradition. He looks in church. He looks in AA. But no lightning bolts strike him. No mountaintop visions appear to him. He becomes discouraged until another AA member reassures him that simply believing there must be a God out there is enough.

Little Tricksters

Be patient, the other member tells him. Keep looking and you'll form a concept of God. It doesn't have to happen in a dramatic fashion. That reassures him.

Then, his life changes with this great, simple prayer he says. One night he feels an irresistible pull toward the party next door. He can't reach his sponsor. He fears he'll drink. So, he sits on his bed and prays to his buddy, God. Nothing formal or fancy. But it's enough to change his life. He's honest. He makes a direct appeal to God for help. He does so in a personal way, with the words that work for him. It's from his heart. And he finds God. A peace comes over him. Not a huge hit of peace, but enough to ease the anxiety and let him enjoy a good night's sleep. He reached out honestly, and God was there. That was enough for him to trust that God would always be there and not let him down.

> The best prayers of recovering people: "Help" and "Thank you."

Studying the Big Book becomes another critical element in his sobriety. He jokes that the *Bugalademujs* (little tricksters) are changing the words to make them more agreeable. The truth is that he becomes open and willing to hear what the book says. That's what helps him make sense of the program's wisdom.

His faith increases and his fears decrease. That's the opposite of what happened when he drank. He finds that faith—not alcohol—cures his insecurities about being different. There's a place in AA for red-headed Native Americans. And they don't have to be tough guys to stay.

In fact, he reveals a soft spot. He sponsors others, passing on what he has been given. This helps him hold on to what he has. And, he says he understands compassion. That's a huge stride: to go from being self-centered to caring how others feel. And his faith—not alcohol—carried him.

17

EMPTY ON THE INSIDE

Anything you put before your sobriety you will lose.

This story, found on page 512, is about a woman who pretends to know what she doesn't. You may recognize yourself. She feels like God gave everyone but her the directions on life. She fears that others will find out what she doesn't know. She desperately wants to escape feeling like an idiot, so she works hard to cover up her weaknesses.

One of her defenses is to show contempt for those who appear to know what they're doing. In other words, she looks down on people who seem above her. It's like the AA saying "An alcoholic is an ego-maniac with an inferiority complex." That describes most of us.

To make up for feeling less than others, we try to make ourselves better than them. I was surprised when my treatment counselor accused me of grandiosity, or putting myself above others. It surprised me because I felt so much less than others. He explained how I used that as a defense, trying to find some way I was better than everybody I met. It was as though I wanted to put them down before they could put me down. That's how I protected my fragile self-esteem.

Like the woman telling her story here, I often fumbled with situations that others seemed to know how to handle. Whether it was talking to girls, trying out for a team, giving a presentation in class, or just making plans for Friday night, I felt ill at ease. Others, though, made doing those things look so easy, as though they'd been given private instructions on how to do them. I, too, worked hard to cover up my insecurity.

As a girl going to AA meetings with her dad, the narrator formed two significant impressions. First, you had to watch how much you reveal about your drinking. If others find out you drink too much, you couldn't drink again and had to attend meetings the rest of your life. So, she learned the importance of hiding her use.

Second, she thought AA was simply a bunch of old guys sitting around eating donuts. Looking back, she realizes that these "old guys" were probably barely thirty, not so old to her now. Even though her two impressions may not have been true, they became beliefs for her.

Her First Love

She remembers the details of her first drunk down to what she was wearing. Alcohol became her first boyfriend. During that first drunk, it was as though her eyes met those of a future lover across the room. And she knew, she just *knew* they'd be happy together. She loved how she changed under alcohol's influence. She became sociable and felt she belonged. While drinking, she didn't think she had to pretend. Of course, while drunk, she wasn't exactly her natural self. But she realized that only later.

After getting drunk for the first time at fifteen, this girl's life falls apart fast. Within a year, she experiences serious consequences in various areas of her life:

- school (grades plunge)
- social (friends change)
- health/safety (wrecks car)
- self-esteem (appearance goes downhill)
- legal (suspended from school)

Remember the *DSM-IV* criteria described in chapter 7? With her drinking altering so many areas of her life, she scores high.

When she gets into trouble with her use, she promises to change. Just like those old guys eating donuts had no doubt done. But alcohol won't let her keep her word. She keeps getting into trouble because of her use.

So Much Promise

She fell short of her potential. Ever hear that? "You're not living up to your potential." Or, "You have so much promise." That seemed to be my theme song. I heard it from a chorus of adults—parents, teachers, coaches, counselors. What was holding me back? Well, I was often stoned instead of studying, practicing, or doing whatever it was I was supposed to be doing. Or, I tried doing those things stoned.

This woman gives two explanations for flunking out of college. First, she skipped class to be with friends. She was afraid that if she didn't, her friends would find out they had a better time without her. Then, they'd reject her, and she'd be left alone and lonely.

Second, she didn't feel confident in her ability to talk to other people. God hadn't given her the instructions on social conversation. But when she drank, alcohol made her social. So she drank too much.

Truth is, she flunked out of college because her insecurities got the better of her. That's what kept her out of class and put a drink in her hand.

She says drinking took her places she never meant to go. She means that physically and emotionally. Physically, she attempted geographics. She headed to other states where she thought she could escape the consequences of her drinking. Emotionally, she wound up in an unhappy marriage. Later, she lost her kids. Drinking transported her to such unhappiness.

She wouldn't admit she was in a bad marriage because she didn't want to have to take responsibility. She didn't want to look honestly at how her drinking distorted her judgment. She didn't want to risk losing her first love. So, she waited for her husband to throw her out. That way, she could blame him. She preferred to blame others rather than take responsibility for her own behavior.

A Low Bottom

After her life crumbles even more, she goes to an AA meeting and admits she's an alcoholic. But that admission isn't enough to stop her negative consequences. She has to stop using first—something she's not quite willing to do yet. She has not yet hit bottom.

The consequences pile up with the divorce, her move home, the arrest for child endangerment, and losing custody of her children. But that isn't bottom enough for her. She keeps drinking.

Drinking has become so important to her that she puts it before her children. She leaves them home alone so she can go out and drink. It's heartbreaking to read. She loves them, but her relationship with alcohol is more important. It really is her first love.

The turning point comes for her one day in her attic apartment. In a daze, not knowing if it's day or night, she feels as cold and gray as the November weather. She sinks to her knees and prays for help. She finds her copy of the Big Book and reads the first chapter. She identifies with Bill W.'s story and is able to get honest with herself. She admits that drinking has ruined her life.

But that honesty is still not enough to keep her from drinking. It's not until she winds up in detox that she hits bottom. That happens when no one shows up to bail her out. The detox counselors refuse her request to be sent to treatment.

Instead, they tell her it's time for her to walk the walk. She must take responsibility for her own life. No one else could get sober for her. She finally becomes accountable for her own recovery.

She took responsibility by doing several things right off. Her first night out of detox, she went to a meeting. She asked a woman with whom she identified to be her sponsor. She attended two meetings daily. She studied the Big Book. In short, she took action rather than waiting for someone else to take it for her. God's grace showed up in her life.

For instance, when she feels left out of the circle during the closing prayer, someone reaches out to her. The AA members act out the AA saying "Whenever anyone anywhere reaches out for help, I want the hand of AA always to be there, and for that I am responsible." She feels God's grace in that.

The Taste of Gratitude

Even though she wasn't excited to attend AA as an adult, the message and wisdom of the program snuck in. She admitted her way wasn't working and became willing to try someone else's way. That was enough to start her off on sobriety.

In AA, she tastes gratitude. When she hears the man speak about his nine-year-old daughter being killed by a drunk driver, she becomes grateful for what she has. She recognizes that her life sober is better than her life drunk.

> Gratitude comes from appreciating what we have, not from getting what we want.

AA gives her the foundation to improve her relationship with her children. Sobriety gives her back the ability to love them and to be reliable. Eventually, it allows her to regain custody. With the help of AA and by God's grace, she becomes fit to be their mother.

She recognizes the source of her strength and love. Even after she remarries, she doesn't lose sight of her priorities. She places God first and AA second. Her husband is never more than the third most important aspect of her life. She has to fill herself up first so that she has something to give others.

She maintains a solid foundation of sobriety. She still has a sponsor. She still has a home group. She still does what works. She sponsors others. She laughs often. She learned how to stay sober, how to be a good parent, and how to be a loving spouse by watching others who did those things well. Their examples finally provided the set of instructions she had been missing.

18

ANOTHER CHANCE

AA is a simple program for complicated people.

On page 531 we meet an African American woman. She offers a simple explanation of her alcoholism. She says she became an alcoholic because she "drank too much too often." She couldn't keep herself from drinking too much. She couldn't stop the problems that drinking too much caused. She did this too often. She was powerless over alcohol. It made her life unmanageable. Pretty simple.

But she blamed her drinking on other circumstances. She blamed it on being poor. I've heard others blame their drinking on their wealthy upbringing. Can't be both, can it? We can turn any circumstance into a scapegoat. Blame it on being black. Blame it on being white. Blame it on your parents. Blame it on your children. Whatever. They're just excuses.

The truth is that drinking problems start with a decision to reach for that first drink. The problems develop for the alcoholic because of a disease. Doesn't matter if you're rich or poor, black or white. If you're an alcoholic, your alcoholic mind can trick you into drinking, and the disease can keep you down. Alcoholism works from the inside out.

This woman hated AA her first time around. She knew that sometimes she drank too much, but she denied that she was an alcoholic. She wasn't like *them*. She felt different. She feared she couldn't live without drinking. She focused on the other alcoholics' outsides, which did indeed look different.

She hit an ugly bottom. As we've seen in the earlier stories of white and Native American alcoholics, she put alcohol before her children. She drank instead of caring for them. She felt so desperate that she tried to kill herself. She killed somebody else while in a blackout. She wound up in prison.

Finally, once she was locked up, she became willing to listen to AA's message. Her way had put her behind bars. Now she was willing to listen to how someone else's way might free her from addiction.

A Second Chance

She believes that she received a second chance with sobriety and with life by the grace of God. This time, she looks for what will bring her together with others rather than what will keep her apart. She focuses on the alcoholic part of her opening statement instead of the African American part. That's not to say she denies her identity. It's just that she's able to see how who she is resembles other addicts. She accepts that she's one of us.

That's how she discovers the solution. By sharing the same disease, we are able to help another alcoholic. Our common experience brings us together. That's how we're able to understand one another. That's how we're able to help one another. That's how we're able to help ourselves. She thanks God for giving her another chance to help other alcoholics, for giving her another chance to help herself.

By identifying with others in AA, she has found friends in the Fellowship. She's found friends who care about who she is, rather than how she looks. She's found that we're all the same color on the inside.

The Fellowship has introduced her to true friends. They don't want something *from* her; they want something *for* her. They want her to stay sober. They're willing to give her their support so she can have that. And she's willing to do the same for them.

It troubles her that more African Americans aren't in the program. Something keeps them away, though she's not sure what. Perhaps it's the same thing that kept her from identifying with the other alcoholics her first time around. This time, however, she's found that she has nothing to fear among her friends in AA.

The Glue That Binds

She feels a part of the Fellowship. She feels accepted as a full member. Other alcoholics treat her like she belongs, which, of course, she does. Maybe that's the key. She isn't waiting for others to say, "We accept you as one of us." She admits, "I am one of you." And that's what makes her a full member in the Fellowship.

She's found the glue that binds us together. We share the same disease. And we share the same solution. By helping one another, we're able to stay sober together.

In recovery, solutions do not come to those who stand still. This is a program of action. We must get out and work it, which includes working with others.

She extends an invitation to her African American brothers and sisters to check out AA. The solution waits for them. Once they've found it works for them, other African Americans wait for them to spread the news. It's as though she says, "Come join me in this life-saving work."

19

FREEDOM FROM BONDAGE

Drinking causes stinking thinking.

They say that our emotional development stops when we begin drinking or drugging heavily. That means that a thirty-year-old man who began smoking dope at thirteen may have outgrown his acne, but he's still a kid when it comes to dealing with his feelings. Once we sober up, it takes awhile for us to mature emotionally.

The woman on page 544 admits up front that her emotional development stopped before she even started drinking. Her *reaction* to her emotions handcuffed her growth. AA taught her how to stop drinking. Perhaps even more important, the program taught her how to deal with her emotions. As she says, AA set her free. It did that by straightening out her thinking.

When she was seven years old, her parents separated. She was sent to live with her grandparents. She felt lonely, terrified, and hurt. Those feelings are normal for a child in that situation. It was her reaction that caused her problems. She decided that she'd never depend upon anybody again. She'd never let herself get close to anyone else. That way, her young mind reasoned, others couldn't hurt her. She would protect herself from future pain.

Later, as a teenager, she felt restless, anxious, scared, and insecure. Sound familiar? Once again, it was her reaction that caused further emotional problems. This time, her emotionally immature mind believed that financial security would wipe out her unpleasant feelings. So, she married a man with a fortune.

An Economic Geographic

You might say that she attempted an economic geographic. She thought if she could only move up the income bracket, she'd feel better. Not so. As with any geographic, she noticed things changed on the outside but not on the inside. Even with money, she felt restless, anxious, scared, and insecure.

Yet she wasn't able to get honest with herself. She blamed her husband, divorced him, and tried another man. Again, she reacted to her emotions rather than deal with them head-on.

This time she married a man other women desired. She thought it would give her self-esteem a boost if an attractive man picked her. Once again, things changed on the outside but not on the inside. She still felt restless, anxious, scared, and insecure.

She divorced him, and her surroundings changed again. Twice divorced and only twenty-three, she added loneliness and hopelessness to her interior landscape. She felt her life lacked a purpose. She felt like a failure.

A Drunken Cocoon

Looking back, she recognizes a "spiritual hunger" that was going unfed. It wasn't until she arrived in AA that she would learn to feed herself spiritually. She hungered for God in her life but couldn't identify the hunger.

Instead, she thirsted for alcohol. When she drank, she didn't feel afraid or any of those other unpleasant emotions that haunted her. She wrapped herself in a drunken cocoon. Resentment and self-pity kept her company.

She admits that she resented just about everyone she knew. Yet what each of her relationships had in common was her. Maybe the problem wasn't that everybody had wronged her. Maybe the problem was her *belief* that everyone had wronged her. Her thinking led to those resentments. Once again, her reaction to situations caused greater misery.

The only people who understood her were other drunks who also felt wronged by everyone they knew. She added remorse, shame, and humiliation to her stockpile of permanent feelings. Feeling lousy whenever sober, she tried to wash away her unhappiness with alcohol. Yet again, her thinking ran funny. She believed she needed to drink to deal with her feelings. She saw alcohol as her hope and her salvation. Not surprisingly, her reaction made her feel worse.

She married for a third time. This time, she thought if she married a man who drank like her, she'd finally be happy. Remember, those who drank like her were the only ones she thought understood her. That idea ended in divorce number three.

She gave marriage yet another try. This time—her fourth—she thought marrying a man with children might save her from drinking so much. She thought the responsibility of caring for children would keep her sober. Wrong again. After three weeks of being a mom, she spent the next two months trying to drink herself to death.

No More Choices

That scared her straight. She wound up in jail and then a psych ward. She had no choice about where the authorities sent her. She realized that practicing alcoholics have no rights. That scared her.

The fear made her open to AA. She was open to finding a way to deal with her emotions. All her life to that point, she had simply reacted to them. She was also open to changing her thinking. Her way hadn't worked, so she was willing to try AA's way.

Here's how she defined her life as unmanageable: She considered where she had planned to be with her life. Then, she looked at where she was. She hadn't wound up where she wanted to go. Her thinking, her reactions to her emotions, and her drinking had blown her life way off course.

That all happened to me in one night. I went to a party and wound up in detox. I hadn't planned that. Looking back, I can see that once I got drunk and high, I couldn't have stopped it from happening. I lost control over the consequences and what happened to me when I used. I was powerless. And my life became unmanageable. So, too, the narrator lost control over the direction of her life.

Finally, she takes the first Step. She admits she's powerless over alcohol and that her life has become unmanageable. Up until then, she had rationalized her problems.

That's pretty typical for an addict or alcoholic. As mentioned in earlier chapters, we rationalize to protect our use. To avoid looking at the actual causes of our problems. We got pretty creative in finding socially acceptable reasons for our socially unacceptable behavior. That's crazy. It's our addict mind acting up. Hello, Step Two.

Life on Life's Terms

She had spent her life trying to escape her feelings. That's how she *reacted*. AA taught her how to deal with feelings and how to deal with life on life's terms. She explains the *HOW* of recovery:

- H for honesty
- O for open-mindedness
- W for willingness

The Big Book calls these three traits the "essentials of recovery."

She became honest, open, and willing. When the members of AA told her to read the Big Book, she did. When they told her to practice the Steps as the Big Book instructed, she did. That's HOW she got sober.

Part of this woman's earlier depression came from a sense of uselessness. She felt her life lacked purpose. AA has given her a sense of purpose. It's also given her serenity, or peace of mind. That's amazing. This is the same woman who had been haunted by anxiety, self-pity, and fear. How did she find serenity?

By working with others, she says. She read the Big Book. She worked the Steps. And she worked with others, just like the Big Book and Step Twelve told her to. That gives her peace of mind. She has come up with a formula that could work for you too. The amount of serenity she brings to others equals the amount she enjoys. Spread the word, and you'll feel peace.

Maybe you've heard people in AA say, "I used to have a drinking problem. Now that I quit drinking, I have a living problem." Take away the alcohol or drugs, and we still have to deal with life. We still have to deal with our emotions and our shortcomings. She says her problems in recovery are caused not by alcohol but by herself. Her self-will may not run riot anymore, but it can still get out of control. That causes her problems and sends her back to work the Steps.

The Mother of All Resentments

Her biggest problem well into sobriety was her resentment against her mother. She knew that resentment would keep her sick. That resentment could make her drink again. But her resentment against her mother was just too big for her to let go of. She was too hurt and angry. That resentment kept her stuck.

If you're struggling with a resentment, try this prayer: "Dear God, please give to [fill in the person's name] all of the good things that I want for myself. Please bring this person health, happiness, and prosperity. Show him or her your love. Amen."

She found a solution in prayer. First, she prayed that God would show her a way to free herself from the bondage of this resentment. Then, she came across the suggestion to pray for the person she resented. For two weeks, she prayed that her mother would be healthy and happy. It worked. She was able to let go of her resentment. Her prayer freed her from the threat to her sobriety.

You can be very specific in your prayers. You can list the

things you want for yourself and ask that God give those things to the other person as well.

The Big Book suggests that if you say this prayer every day for two weeks, you'll no longer feel resentment. Your hatred and bitterness will change to love and compassion. If that doesn't happen after two weeks, say the prayer for another two weeks. Really mean it. This woman claims saying that prayer has worked for her many times. I believe her. It's worked for me too. And it's worked for many others I know in AA.

If at first you just can't bring yourself to pray for good things to happen to the person you resent, start by praying for the willingness to say the prayer. After a few days, you'll likely be able to pray for good things to come his or her way. Freeing yourself of resentments will make room for serenity.

This woman has grown up in AA. Even though she was thirty-three when she arrived, she dealt with her emotions like a little girl. The program let her mature. She's been honest and open about her shortcomings. She's been willing to change. And she has changed—for the better. Once lonely, terrified, and hurt, she's now happy, joyous, and free.

The Twelve Steps of Alcoholics Anonymous*

1. We admitted we were powerless over alcohol—that our lives had become unmanageable.
2. Came to believe that a Power greater than ourselves could restore us to sanity.
3. Made a decision to turn our will and our lives over to the care of God *as we understood Him.*
4. Made a searching and fearless moral inventory of ourselves.
5. Admitted to God, to ourselves, and to another human being the exact nature of our wrongs.
6. Were entirely ready to have God remove all these defects of character.
7. Humbly asked Him to remove our shortcomings.
8. Made a list of all persons we had harmed, and became willing to make amends to them all.
9. Made direct amends to such people wherever possible, except when to do so would injure them or others.
10. Continued to take personal inventory and when we were wrong promptly admitted it.
11. Sought through prayer and meditation to improve our conscious contact with God *as we understood Him,* praying only for knowledge of His will for us and the power to carry that out.
12. Having had a spiritual awakening as the result of these steps, we tried to carry this message to alcoholics, and to practice these principles in all our affairs.

---

* From *Alcoholics Anonymous*, 4th ed., published by AA World Services, Inc., New York, N.Y., 59–60.

ABOUT THE AUTHOR

John R. sobered up at seventeen, before he was old enough to legally drink. Over twenty years of continuous sobriety, he has worked as a chemical dependency counselor with young people in high schools and residential treatment centers. He also has written extensively on the subject of adolescent addiction and recovery. He lives in Minneapolis with his wife and their two children, but calls his Thursday night AA group home.

Hazelden, a national nonprofit organization founded in 1949, helps people reclaim their lives from the disease of addiction. Built on decades of knowledge and experience, Hazelden offers a comprehensive approach to addiction that addresses the full range of patient, family, and professional needs, including treatment and continuing care for youth and adults, research, higher learning, public education and advocacy, and publishing.

A life of recovery is lived "one day at a time." Hazelden publications, both educational and inspirational, support and strengthen lifelong recovery. In 1954, Hazelden published *Twenty-Four Hours a Day,* the first daily meditation book for recovering alcoholics, and Hazelden continues to publish works to inspire and guide individuals in treatment and recovery, and their loved ones. Professionals who work to prevent and treat addiction also turn to Hazelden for evidence-based curricula, informational materials, and videos for use in schools, treatment programs, and correctional programs.

Through published works, Hazelden extends the reach of hope, encouragement, help, and support to individuals, families, and communities affected by addiction and related issues.

For questions about Hazelden publications,
please call **800-328-9000**
or visit us online at **hazelden.org/bookstore.**

1-4-18
1-27-20-2-1022
41   5 (CLAy)